TOWNS ON THE WILD ATLANTIC WAY

FROM DONEGAL TO CORK

Richard Butler

THE O'BRIEN PRESS
DUBLIN

ABOUT THE AUTHOR

Richard Butler is a historian of modern Ireland and Director of Research at Mary Immaculate College (MIC) in Limerick. He grew up in Bantry in west Cork and holds a PhD in Architectural History from the University of Cambridge. A keen hiker, cyclist and sailor, Richard has extensive first-hand knowledge of the entire Wild Atlantic Way from land and sea, and combines this with academic expertise in Ireland's history and culture. His publications include *Building the Irish Courthouse and Prison: A Political History, 1750–1850* (Cork University Press, 2020) and the edited collection *Dreams of the Future in Nineteenth-Century Ireland* (Liverpool University Press, 2021).

The twelve-arch stone railway viaduct at Ballydehob.

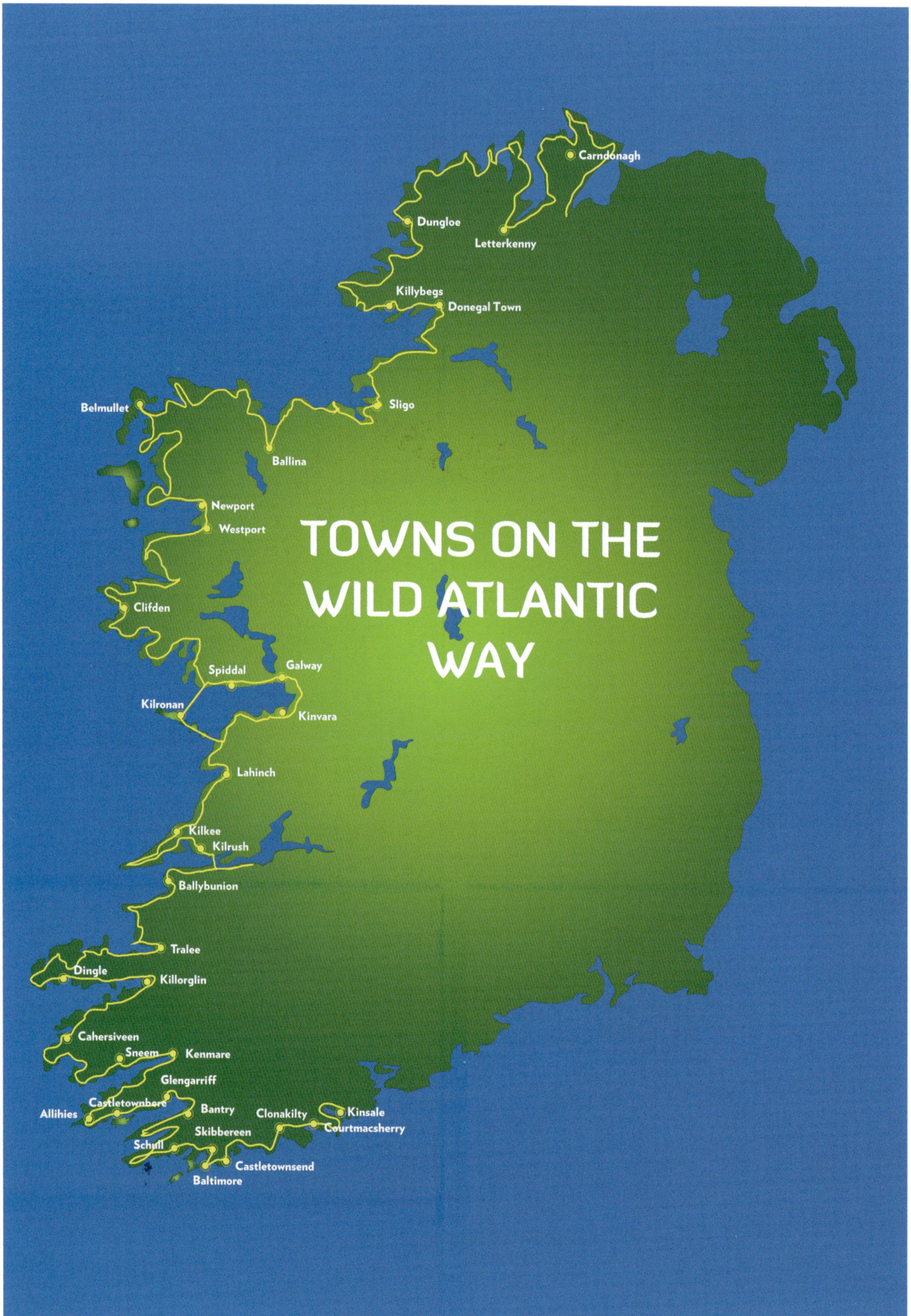
TOWNS ON THE WILD ATLANTIC WAY
Carndonagh
Dungloe
Letterkenny
Killybegs
Donegal Town
Sligo
Belmullet
Ballina
Newport
Westport
Clifden
Spiddal
Galway
Kilronan
Kinvara
Lahinch
Kilkee
Kilrush
Ballybunion
Tralee
Dingle
Killorglin
Cahersiveen
Sneem
Kenmare
Glengarriff
Castletownbere
Allihies
Bantry
Clonakilty
Kinsale
Courtmacsherry
Skibbereen
Schull
Castletownsend
Baltimore

Fanad lighthouse.

Westport.

Dunguaire Castle, near Kinvara.

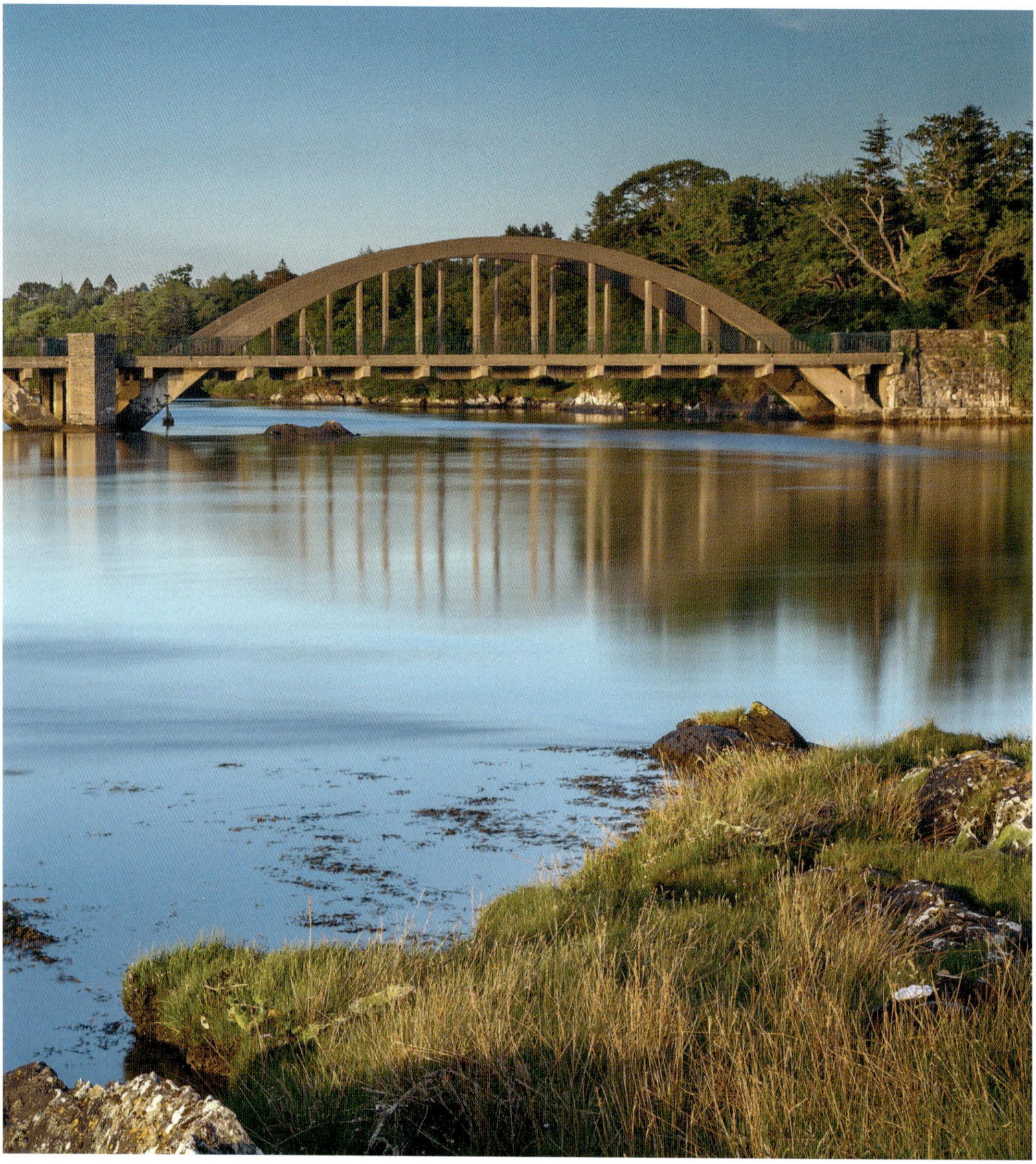

Kenmare.

Inchydoney beach.

Blennerville, near Tralee.

INTRODUCTION

When I first read about the launch of the Wild Atlantic Way (*Slí an Atlantaigh Fhiáin*) route back in 2014, I knew it would be an instant success. It made so much sense to someone who grew up by the sea in Bantry, and who has spent so many years exploring the southwest on foot, on two wheels and on four, and under sail. Of course, tourism was far from new to the west of Ireland, but the route somehow brought everything together. The name, too, goes back a long way – two hundred years ago, English tourists travelled along the coastline admiring 'the wilds of Connamara' (John Trotter, 1817) and writing books such as *Wild Sports of the West of Ireland* (William Maxwell, 1832). Many of them had read Sydney Owenson's *The Wild Irish Girl* (1806) and were as interested in finding 'wild' people as they were in exploring wild landscapes. Ever since, tourism in Ireland has been synonymous with the magic of the western coastline, whether in John Ford's Hollywood films or in the escape to Achill chronicled in Heinrich Böll's *Irisches Tagebuch* (1957).

The 2,500km-long Wild Atlantic Way brought with it a new way of thinking about this coastline. It tied together all the headlands and the islands, the mountains and the rivers, the castles, the big houses, the harbours, the ruins old and new, and much more besides. And it tied together the towns and the cities. Too often, places like Bantry tended to be overlooked in guides or mentioned only in passing. Visitors were implored to see a particular mountain, lighthouse, or beach – and who wouldn't want to see these? But sometimes this relegated the towns to second fiddle, to be experienced only through a car window while driving to the next tourist sight.

My travels along the western seaboard while researching this book convinced me that to bypass the towns was to miss out on so much of what makes the Wild Atlantic Way so special. My idea, then, was to bring the towns into central focus and write a guide that gave something of their history, their festivals, and their traditions. Perhaps half a million people have the privilege of living on or near Ireland's western coastline – with the majority living in the thirty or so largest cities and towns. In this book, I suggest that visitors might choose to take accommodation in these cities and towns while exploring the Wild Atlantic Way. Rather than proposing daytrips *to* the nearest town, this book hints at what can be seen on days out *from* these towns. The reader will discover that all of the most famous sights associated with the route are within a half-hour's drive of one of these towns.

This guide is intended for the kind of person who enjoys wandering around a town and learning something about it. And there is something comforting about a town-centre guestroom, especially after a day out in the countryside. You can park your car, put away your bike, or just clean your muddy boots, and wander out for a great dinner or a few pints. As you'll discover, many of Ireland's Atlantic towns come to life after sunset. In the warm summer months, some places keep going all night too.

A NOTE ON NAMING CONVENTIONS

Towns and attractions situated within Gaeltacht areas are referred to in this book by their Irish-language names first, with English translations following in brackets.

Carndonagh
Dungloe
Letterkenny
Killybegs
Donegal Town

Malin Head on the Inishowen Peninsula is the most northerly point on the island of Ireland.

CARNDONAGH AND THE INISHOWEN PENINSULA

If you have committed to the entire Wild Atlantic Way, the Inishowen Peninsula will be either the beginning or the end of your trip. I would recommend it as your starting point: it's close to a big city (Derry) yet overwhelmingly rural, it's packed full of history and culture, and the weather will gradually improve as you head south!

CARNDONAGH (*CARN DOMHNACH*), often shortened to just 'Carn', means 'the mound of the church' in Irish. Though an ancient name, it remains a perfect description for the place: as you approach the town, you will see an enormous stone-clad Catholic church, built in the 1940s atop a hill. Truly it dominates the skyline with its conservative neo-Romanesque architecture, and keen observers will not be surprised to read that it was one of the inspirations for Galway Cathedral some years later.

The town almost plays second-fiddle to this vast church. Home to around 2,500 people, Carndonagh has a nice, neat triangular centre with old pubs and useful shops. A little west, beyond the bridge over the Donagh river, is a religious site of national importance: under a wooden shelter next to Donagh Church (Church of Ireland) is St Patrick's High Cross. Flanked by two carved pillar stones, this High Cross has a depiction of Christ beneath interlace patterns and is believed to date from the seventh century (and so perhaps within two centuries of St Patrick's death).

Inishowen's remarkably rich history goes back many centuries and is celebrated during the Colgan Heritage Weekend. Staged in the town each June, the weekend is named after another prominent religious figure, Fr John Colgan (c. 1590–1658), a Franciscan friar who became a leading theologian on the continent.

It is also a peninsula that has, in recent years, attracted artists and musicians who have added to its cultural richness. The Inishowen Gospel Choir, for example, founded in 2005, performs internationally, while the Silver Birch Gallery & Studio, near Carndonagh, showcases Sharon McDaid's paintings of the local landscape.

Carndonagh makes for an ideal base to explore the whole area, including:

Doagh Famine Village, Lagacurry, a 15-minute drive. A folk museum showcasing traditional nineteenth-century Donegal housing and exploring the Great Famine (guided tours available). Adjacent are peaceful sandy beaches.

Buncrana (*Bun Cranncha*), a 20-minute drive. Inishowen's biggest town (population: 3,400). Dating back to the medieval period, Buncrana became a popular holiday destination for daytrippers from Derry in the Victorian era, while also maintaining a proud textile industry. It is still a popular spot for seaside walks.

Greencastle (*An Caisleán Nua*), a 20-minute drive. Strategically located to defend Lough Foyle, this place is home to a ruined Norman-era castle and a fort built during the Napoleonic Wars. The harbour is busy with fishing boats and the ferry to Magilligan. The Inishowen Maritime Museum & Planetarium is worth a visit.

Malin Head (*Cionn Mhálanna*), a 25-minute drive. This is the most northerly point on the island of Ireland. Though it is less dramatic than Mizen Head, you will find an old signal tower here.

Fort Dunree (*An Dún Riabhach*), a 30-minute drive. Dramatically sited on cliffs overlooking Lough Swilly, it is now home to an extensive military museum. Lough Swilly was one of the 'treaty ports' handed back to the Free State in 1938, and Fort Dunree was where the official ceremony took place.

Burt (*An Bheart*, also known as Speenoge), a 30-minute drive. Perhaps the greatest of Liam McCormick's modernist churches, St Aengus (1967) combines the old and the new; its interior is the work of a gifted architect at the peak of his creativity.

IMAGES Top: The old signal tower at Malin Head. Middle left: Built atop a hill, Sacred Heart Church dominates the Carndonagh skyline. Middle right: Dramatic lighting inside St Aengus's Church (1967), designed by Liam McCormick. Bottom: The bridge over the River Crana near Buncrana Castle.

Derry (*Doire*), a 35-minute drive. Derry, home to more than 90,000 people, and the fifth largest city on the island of Ireland, is *not* part of the Wild Atlantic Way route. This makes little sense to me, but perhaps Inishowen will seem to many visitors to be a natural end-point for their journey. Yet if you make it as far as the Donegal–Derry border, it really is worth spending at least a couple of days getting to know Derry's rich culture and complicated history. After all, Derry is known as the last walled city that was built in Europe (completed in 1619). Here too begins the Causeway Coastal Route along the north Ulster coastline.

LETTERKENNY

LETTERKENNY (*LEITIR CEANAINN*). 'Hillside of the O'Cannons' is what Letterkenny's name means in Irish, and it remains an accurate description today. What was originally a single street leading to a bridge over the River Swilly has now swelled to a large and sprawling town, with new housing estates climbing up and over the surrounding hills. As with Newry in County Down, you see the town long before you get to its centre. Letterkenny is the largest town in Donegal and, in many ways, its

Top: Derry is the last walled city that was built in Europe.
Bottom: Urban skyline of Derry with its famous Peace Bridge.

The Letterkenny skyline is dominated by the Roman Catholic Cathedral of St Eunan.

administrative centre (though the much smaller Lifford to the south is the official old 'county town'). Home to around 20,000 people, it vies with Sligo as the third largest town on the Wild Atlantic Way. Here you will find the Letterkenny Institute of Technology and all the services you would expect for such a large town.

Letterkenny is set back a little from the sea and certainly doesn't feel like a coastal town. A few kilometres downstream is the glacial fjord of Lough Swilly, which opens up majestically north of Rathmullan. Like Berehaven, this stretch of water was one of the 'treaty ports' given over to the Irish Free State in 1938 (see the section on Carndonagh, p.14). Letterkenny, as a land-locked market town, dates back much further: it was founded during the Ulster Plantation of the seventeenth century. In 1798, a French force attempted to land nearby but was intercepted by the British Royal Navy (see also Ballina, p.30, and Bantry, pp. 90-91). Among the French sailors was Theobald Wolfe Tone (1763–1798), who was arrested and held briefly at Laird's Hotel in Letterkenny before being moved on to Derry Gaol. He was later convicted and soon after took his own life.

Letterkenny is known by many locals as 'the cathedral town', for it is the seat of the Catholic bishop of Raphoe. The great spire of St Eunan's, built in the 1890s, is visible for many kilometres around; inside there are stained-glass windows by Michael Healy (in the transepts, 1910–1911), and by Harry Clarke (in the clerestory, 1928–1929). Near the cathedral is the attractive, tree-lined market square – a relaxing place to sit and enjoy the goings-on in the town. The square opens onto Main Street, the central artery of the town, where you will find all the best pubs and restaurants.

Where Main Street turns into High Road is the Donegal County Museum (free admission) housed in part of the old workhouse, and nearby the Regional Cultural Centre and An Grianán Theatre – whose music and shows draw large crowds from all across the northwest. For daytrips further beyond:

Raphoe (*Ráth Bhoth*), a 15-minute drive. Home to a Church of Ireland cathedral. At the edge of the town is the Oakfield Park Estate, an immaculate Georgian country house with landscaped gardens and woods. Also, 3.5km south of the town is the Beltany Stone Circle, consisting of sixty-four standing stones dating from perhaps 2000BC.

Glenveagh National Park, a 25-minute drive. In the general vicinity of Errigal (see Dungloe, p.19). An old estate with a castle, gardens, and woods, opening onto Lough Beagh and a great, empty valley.

Top: Fanad lighthouse at sunset.
Left: The landmark chimney at Sion Mills, built in 1877.
Above: The busy Main Street of Dungloe.

Sion Mills, Co. Tyrone, a 30-minute drive. Like Saltaire or New Lanark, Sion Mills was built as a utopian industrial town. The Herdman family began their project in 1835. Today, with its enormous factory buildings and great chimney (from 1877), the site is quite a contrast to the typical Donegal rural landscape. The whole establishment closed in 2004 and is, at the time of writing, derelict. Nearby, in better condition, is the modernist St Teresa's Church (1963, by Patrick Haughey), from which an enormous slate sculpture of the Last Supper (by Oisín Kelly) looks onto the main road.

Dunfanaghy (*Dún Fionnachaidh*, 'fort of the fair field'), a 35-minute drive. Known for its many fine beaches.

Fánaid (*Fanad*), a 50-minute drive. In the Donegal Gaeltacht. The Fanad Peninsula is situated to the west of Lough Swilly; at its headland is a lighthouse (built in 1886) surrounded by rocky inlets and offering panoramic views.

DUNGLOE

NA CLOCHÁN LIATH (*DUNGLOE*). I don't think that towns loom large in anyone's imagination of northwest Donegal: this is a landscape of desolate emptiness and, where humans have intruded, of small clusters of cottages. Na Clochán Liath ('the grey stepping-stones'), also known as Dungloe, is one of the only towns in the area, home to around 1,200 people. Like Waterville in County Kerry, it is built between the sea and a large lake, though unlike its Iveragh cousin its main street faces inwards. The town's name derives from an old fording of a river, the Abhainn na Clochán Liath.

The town is proudly situated in the Donegal Gaeltacht and was founded back in the mid-eighteenth century. At its core, it is a single wide street – straight and planned in a county of few such luxuries. Locals will tell you that it is the capital of Na Rosa ('The Rosses'), a part of Donegal with its own distinctive culture and traditions. The political activist and writer Peadar O'Donnell (1893–1986) was born here, and so too, though no relation, was the singer Daniel O'Donnell (b. 1961). For those keen on the outdoors, the district is perfect for fishing: to the north and east are over a hundred small, peaceful, and picturesque lakes, stocked mostly with trout. Permits are available from the Rosses Angling Association (enquire in the town), and boat hire can also be organised.

Na Clochán Liath has all the shops and services that you would expect for a market town serving a large rural area. And like much of rural Ireland it has had its ups and downs over the years, with emigration still a big concern. One thing, though, that has kept going throughout is the 'Mary from Dungloe International Arts Festival', which is staged each July, and which reflects the theme of emigration. Dating back to the 1960s, it is broadly similar to the 'Rose of Tralee' festival (see Tralee, p.65). 'Marys' from all over the Irish world take part in the competition; at the time of writing, the reigning 'Mary from Dungloe' is Róisín Maher, from County Carlow, who represented New York.

There is a huge amount to explore beyond the town, including:

Ailt an Chorráin (*Burtonport*), a 10-minute drive. Founded in the late eighteenth century to take advantage of the fishing riches of the area, and named after the aristocrat involved, William Burton Conyngham (1733–1796), who happened to own the harp that appears in the Guinness logo. Between 1903 and 1940, the village was the terminus of a remarkable narrow-gauge railway through the mountains from Letterkenny, built to aid the exports of fish.

Árainn Mhór (*Arranmore*). Not to be confused with the Aran Islands. Árainn Mhór is a 20-minute ferry trip from Burtonport and is filled with walking trails on quiet roads. On the western side you'll find cliffs, caves, and a lighthouse.

An Earagail (*Errigal*), a 20-minute drive. The highest point in Donegal at 751m. A dramatic conical peak of quartzite with excellent trails. To the south of the peak is the gaunt ruin of the former Dunlewy church, and further south again, the barren, rocky, foreboding Poisoned Glen. Despite the astonishing remoteness of this place, Donegal Airport, with daily flights to Dublin, and often voted one of the most scenically located airports in the world, is only a 20-minute drive away.

Toraigh (*Tory Island*), a 30-minute drive to the pier at Magheraroarty, and then a 45-minute ferry journey. Ireland's most remote inhabited island, with a permanent population of around 120, Toraigh is often cut off for days in winter storms. Its residents vote early in elections to make sure that the ballots reach the mainland on time. Among all the cliffs and crashing waves, look out for the remains of St Columcille's monastery. Beyond Toraigh there's only Rockall, then Iceland.

KILLYBEGS

KILLYBEGS (*NA CEALLA BEAGA*). I felt lazy wandering around Killybegs on a wet April morning. The town's business is fishing, and the locals were busy coming and going, back on shore after a tough few days spent out in the big swells, or just finished a shift at one of the enormous fish processing factories. Killybegs is Ireland's premier fishing port, and if Donegal Town is something like Bantry, then this place is the Castletownbere of the north. Like all fishing towns its fortunes have gone up and down over the years; in recent times the port has expanded to cater for the importation of giant wind turbines, and tourism, of course, is growing steadily.

Killybegs is an old plantation town, given its charter back in 1616. Its Irish name, *Na Cealla Beaga*, 'the small churches', derives from an early monastic settlement. Today most of the buildings you see date from the nineteenth and twentieth centuries, but near the southernmost quay look out for the scant remains of the unromantic 'Cat Castle', and nearby an old holy well, a grotto, and a ruined church. The ensemble is surrounded by the perimeter fencing of the latest additions to the harbour and a dozen fish factories set into the surrounding hills.

Like its twin in west Cork, Killybegs is reassuringly unpretentious and a welcome antidote to the more pre-packaged tourist sites on the Wild Atlantic Way. Home to around 1,200 people, its other traditional source of employment was in carpet making. On the Fintra Road, in an old factory building, is the Maritime & Heritage Visitor Centre, which explores the legacies of this industry. You will find that most of the town's pubs and restaurants are located on the one-way Main Street: here you can taste some of the freshest seafood you'll find on the entire coastline, and Hughie's Bar is especially recommended for good pints.

As well as hosting the giant trawlers, the quays are now the departure point for organised sea-angling trips, as well as cruises to see the Sliabh Liag cliffs (see below). For a town so attached to the sea, you won't be surprised to read that the main festival, held in August – the Killybegs Summer Street Festival – includes a traditional 'Blessing of the Boats' ritual.

For daytrips beyond Killybegs, see in particular:

Fintragh beach, a 5-minute drive. A Blue Flag beach very close to Killybegs, Fintragh is free of all the industrial fishing activity.

Sliabh Liag, a 30-minute drive. Ireland's highest sea cliffs (600m), comparable only to the north-western edge of Achill Island. Its name, appropriately, translates as 'mountain of stones'. The Pilgrim Path offers a nice hiking route away from the camper vans.

An Trá Bhán (*Silver Strand beach*), Málainn Bhig (*Malin Beg*), a 40-minute drive. This fantastic south-facing beach is locked between high hills.

Gleann Cholm Cille (*Glencolumbkille*), a 30-minute drive. Situated in this remote village in the Donegal Gaeltacht, the Folk Village Museum, established by the celebrated local priest, Fr James McDyer (1910–1987), tells the history of the area.

Na Gleannta ('the glens', *Glenties*), a 30-minute drive. A town of 800 people at the edge of the Donegal Gaeltacht, Glenties holds the record for winning the Irish Tidy Towns Competition more often than any other town. St Conal's Catholic Church (built in the mid-1970s) is one of architect Liam McCormick's most graceful designs. The large cross on the main altar is by the German-Irish sculptor Imogen Stuart. The town is a great place to embark on a classic cycling loop (90km) on quiet roads through valleys. Head for Doocharry, then onwards to Glendowan, turn south to Cloghan, and return to Glenties.

An Port (*Port*), a 50-minute drive. This is a remarkably empty valley with abandoned old stone houses opening on to a majestic, wild bay with crashing waves and cliffs.

IMAGES Top: Fishing trawlers at Killybegs Harbour.
Middle left: The interior of St Conal's Catholic Church in Glenties, showing the cross by Imogen Stuart.
Middle right: Sliabh Liag, Ireland's highest sea cliffs.
Bottom left: An Trá Bhán/Silver Strand beach is surrounded by green hills.

IMAGES Top left: Rolling waves at the vast Rossnowlagh beach. This photo was taken by John Langford, a British tourist, in August 1959; the beautiful landscape is much the same now, more than 60 years later.
Top right: Donegal Castle, showing its early seventeenth-century additions.
Middle left: Bundoran beach.
Middle right: Statue of musician Rory Gallagher in Ballyshannon.
Bottom left: Enniskillen Castle stands on the banks of Lough Erne.

DONEGAL TOWN

If you're driving north along the Wild Atlantic Way from Sligo into Donegal, you will notice a shift in the landscape, and with it, to some extent, comes a change in history and in culture. Donegal is one of the most magical, sparsely populated, and off-the-beaten-track counties in Ireland. It is in the province of Ulster but not in Northern Ireland, connected to the rest of the Republic by a thin sliver of land just 7km from sea to the Fermanagh border. It is hard to overstate how remote and distant Donegal is from Dublin and even more so from the southwest: Malin Head to Mizen Head will take you at least 8½ hours to drive some 600km (it's a classic multi-day cycle). Moreover, Donegal's obvious urban centre – Derry – has for a century been cut off by an international boundary. Too often forgotten as the most northern part of 'the south', Donegal has always struck me as a place that has done its own thing against significant adversity, preserving along the way a special warmth and friendliness.

DONEGAL TOWN (***DÚN NA NGALL***, 'fort of the foreigners'). Though no longer the administrative centre for the county, Donegal Town, is a historic settlement with architecture to prove it. Now home to around 2,600 people, Donegal was the capital of the Gaelic kingdom of Tír Chonaill between the 1470s and the wars of the early 1600s. The O'Donnells built their proud castle around 1505 at a bend on the River Eske near the sea, around which their town developed. With the collapse of the old Gaelic world, the town became part of the Ulster Plantation under Basil Brooke, who extended the old castle in 1610 with a Jacobean-style fortified house featuring an elaborately carved stone fireplace. Partially restored in recent times, it is well worth a visit. Brooke also laid out a classic 'plantation' town, centred on what is still known as 'The Diamond'.

Opening onto a large bay and surrounded by mountains, Donegal is somewhat reminiscent of Bantry in the far south-west. Its uplands – the Bluestack Mountains (*Na Cruacha Gorma*, 'the blue stacks') – rise to 674m and separate the southern part of the county from Letterkenny. The dramatic Barnesmore Gap (N15 route) runs through them, linking the town with Ballybofey, and making for an excellent drive. As well as plenty of hiking, the River Eske (*Abhainn na hlascaigh*, 'the river of the fish') is well-known for salmon and trout fishing in the spring and summer. At Lough Eske you will find the ruins of an O'Donnell castle and countless woodland trails.

In the town, along with the castle and the ruins of an old Franciscan friary associated with the landmark text *The Annals of the Four Masters* (1630s), you will find the Donegal Railway Heritage Centre, commemorating the former headquarters of an extensive narrow-gauge network.

The local Catholic church, too, is worth a visit: it has a remarkable 1930s revival of a traditional medieval Round Tower.

The main local arts and music festival – the Donegal Town Summer Festival – takes place each June. In recent years, the town has become an increasingly popular tourist destination, highlighted in several international guides. As well as classic drives, trails, and fishing, there is:

Rossnowlagh beach, a 20-minute drive. There are many great beaches in County Donegal but this Blue Flag surfing beach is undoubtedly my favourite.

The Rory Gallagher International Tribute Festival, Ballyshannon, a 20-minute drive. Ballyshannon is another 'plantation' town and marks an important crossing of the River Erne (now the site of a hydro-electric power station). Home to 2,300 people, Ballyshannon is the birthplace of the guitarist and songwriter Rory Gallagher (1948–1995, buried in Cork). His statue is in the town centre.

Bundoran (*Bun Dobhráin*), a 25-minute drive. When the Dublin railway reached here in the 1860s, so did the sunbathers, and, in more recent years, the surfers too. There are many walking trails by the sea.

Enniskillen (*Inis Ceithleann*), a 55-minute drive. The county town of Fermanagh, and home to an imposing castle dating mostly from the sixteenth century, Enniskillen now has a population of 14,000. Upper and Lower Lough Erne are a boater's paradise.

Belmullet
Sligo
Ballina
Newport
Westport
Clifden
Spiddal

SLIGO TO SPIDDAL

Classiebawn Castle, Mullaghmore, framed by the dramatic Ben Bulben.

SLIGO (*SLIGEACH*, 'ABOUNDING IN SHELLS')

For me, Sligo is all about Ben Bulben, the dramatic flat-topped hill to the north that rises to 526m. Wandering around the town, it is always there, coming in and out of view, appearing at street corners especially near Harmony Hill. Few Irish towns have such a majestic natural monument on their horizon – and one that constantly reminds you of the unique landscape of the area. Though the Wild Atlantic Way route suggests a coastal drive, the best way to arrive in Sligo is on the Dublin train: like Westport or Ballina, it is the final stop, the end of the journey. Having traversed the flat pasturelands and lakes of the north midlands, the end of the railway marks the beginning of the mountains and the ocean.

IMAGES Top left: Sligo streetscape with Ben Bulben in the distance.
Bottom left: The ruins of a thirteenth-century Dominican friary can be seen on Sligo's Abbey Street.
Above: Megalithic tomb and stone circle at Carrowmore.

Sligo is home to almost 20,000 people, making it the joint-third-largest town (with Letterkenny) on the entire route, after Galway and Tralee. In recent years, with improved roads, Sligo has become a fashionable place to escape to from the capital and live a more rural life, and it is now a remarkably international place with, among others, a large Polish community. It is also a town known for music: the Sligo Jazz Project in July, the Sligo Festival of Baroque Music in September, and the Sligo Live Festival in October.

Sligo makes places like Cahersiveen or Clifden seem like they were founded only yesterday. All around the town are prehistoric archaeological sites of international importance (see below), of a density comparable only to the Boyne valley in County Meath. The town itself dates roughly from the thirteenth century (the Norman era), and it developed along the southern banks of the short Garavoge river, which drains from Lough Gill. On Abbey Street, look out for the extensive and well-preserved ruins of a Dominican friary founded in the 1250s, including a tower, a cloister, and a church with lots of tall, thin lancet windows.

From more recent times, the remains of the old county jail still survive; the jail was closed in the late 1950s. Here the revolutionary Michael Collins was sentenced to three weeks' solitary confinement in 1918 (about which he kept a diary). For architecture enthusiasts, the Victorian-era courthouse and town hall buildings are both well worth visiting, as is the vast Catholic cathedral, built in the 1870s. The railway station, too, is unusually grand, perched high over the town like a little stone version of Ben Bulben.

It's hard to pick just a few of the dozens of remarkable places to visit beyond the town, but the highlights must surely include:

Carrowmore Tombs (*An Cheathrú Mhór*, 'the great quarter'), a 10-minute drive. This Neolithic treasure-trove of tombs and monuments, is now in the care of the state. Nearby, to the west, you can hike Knocknarea (327m) and explore Queen Maeve's Grave. Carrowmore and Sceilg Mhichíl (see the chapter on Cahersiveen) are the two most important archaeological sites on the entire Wild Atlantic Way.

St Columba's Church, Drumcliff, a 10-minute drive. Known by every Irish schoolchild and all around the world as the burial place of the poet William Butler Yeats (1865–1939). Appropriately enough, the last three lines of his poem 'Under Ben Bulben' are inscribed on the gravestone: 'Cast a cold Eye / On Life, on Death. / Horseman, pass by.'

Rosses Point, a 15-minute drive. Here sand and rolling waves stretch as far as you can see.

Lissadell House, a 20-minute drive. Famous for its Yeatsian connections, Lissadell now boasts a museum, guided tours, and a magnificent walled garden.

Ben Bulben (*Binn Ghulbain*), a 20-minute drive. Visible from all around, Ben Bulben is the most famous hill in the Dartry range. There are dramatic cliffs and waterfalls on the northern side near Gleniff.

Mullaghmore Head, a 25-minute drive. Mullaghmore is a small fishing village well known by surfers for its big Atlantic swells. The horizon is pierced by the turret of Classiebawn, a Scottish Baronial-style Victorian castle built in the 1870s.

IMAGES Top: Headstone of W.B. Yeats in Drumcliff churchyard.
Above: Parke's Castle on the shores of Lough Gill.
Opposite top: A statue at Rosses Point commemorates those lost at sea.
Right: An abandoned house at Gleniff under Ben Bulben.

Lough Gill, a 25-minute drive. This lake can be found in the heart of 'Yeats Country'. The seventeenth-century Parke's Castle is well worth a visit, as is Yeats's little Isle of Inishfree. The N16 drive from Manorhamilton to Sligo is undoubtedly the best approach to either town but is often overlooked.

BALLINA

BALLINA (*BÉAL AN ÁTHA*). Ballina, like Galway, is defined by its relationship to a mighty river that rushes through it from lake to sea. Its Irish name, *Béal an Átha*, 'mouth of the ford', speaks volumes. Home now to 10,200 people, Ballina was for many years the largest town in Mayo but today has been overtaken by Castlebar. It offers the only crossing point for many kilometres of the River Moy, which drains from the vast Lough Conn inland. After heavy rains, the Moy is a sight to behold and is famous for its salmon. In drier times, look out for the anglers standing in the shallows and near what is known locally as the 'Ridge Pool'. For many years, the Republic of Ireland's former soccer manager, Jack Charleton (1935–2020) visited the town and fished here.

Two road bridges and a pedestrian bridge span the Moy, with most of the historic district to the west of the river. Ballina is steeped in history, perhaps most famously for its capture by French forces in 1798 (see Killala, p.32). To the north of the town centre, you will find the Humbert Monument, commemorating the French general in charge, and many of the town's streets are named after prominent figures from the

great Irish rebellion of that year. In local folklore, these events are known simply as *Bliain na bhFrancach*, 'the Year of the French'. The rebellion was, ultimately, unsuccessful, and British control of the area rumbled on until 1921. From more recent times, the town is known as the birthplace of the first woman to be President of Ireland, Mary Robinson (b. 1944), who was elected in 1990.

As a relatively large town in the west of Ireland, Ballina has its fair share of interesting historic buildings, including an old courthouse, churches, and, of course, its graceful stone bridges. The Catholic cathedral of St. Muredach was built in the mid-nineteenth century and is situated on the eastern side of the river; it has an elaborate Gothic interior.

One of the most popular times to visit the town is in July, when the annual Ballina Salmon Festival (*Féile na mBradán*) takes places over eight days. Established more than fifty years ago, this is a major cultural, artistic, and musical event in the west of Ireland. The town also has its fair share of traditional pubs, of which Harrison's, the Auld Shebeen, and Dillon's, are highly recommended. A few minutes' walk north of the town centre brings you to the Connacht Whiskey Company, where tastings and tours are offered.

Ballina is well served by road, rail, and air links, and makes for an ideal base for exploring Mayo. Beyond the town itself, you will find:

Belleek Castle, a 5-minute drive to the north of the town. Built in the 1820s, Belleek is a Gothic fantasy country house that now boasts a museum, a bistro, and extensive woods and trails.

Rosserk Friary, a 15-minute drive. This excellent example of a Franciscan friary was founded around 1440 and burned in 1590. The friars certainly knew how to pick a good site, as Rosserk is superbly located right by the shores of the Moy.

IMAGES Opposite, top: The dramatic River Moy at Ballina.
Opposite, bottom: The Gothic Revival interior of St Muredach's Cathedral, built in the nineteenth century.
Above: The River Moy flows past the remains of Rosserk Friary.

Killala, a 15-minute drive. A village of some 600 people situated where the Moy enters the sea. In the centre look out for the 25m-high medieval Round Tower. Nearby is the wonderful St. Patrick's Cathedral (Church of Ireland) with its bare-stone interior and array of nineteenth-century memorials. As mentioned above, the French under General Humbert landed near Killala in 1798 and marched onwards to Castlebar.

Enniscrone beach, a 15-minute drive. On the eastern shore of the Moy estuary, this is one of the classic sandy beaches of the west of Ireland. It is also home to a links golf course.

Foxford Woollen Mills, a 15-minute drive. Foxford is a small village on the banks of the Moy near Lough Cullin. Since the late nineteenth century, it has been home to a large woollen mill, which now offers tours and a large shop.

Downpatrick Head and **Dún Briste** sea stack, a 35-minute drive. Cliffs and a sea stack showcasing

the interesting geology of the north Mayo coastline. A large 'Éire' sign dates from the Second World War.

BELMULLET

BÉAL AN MHUIRTHEAD (*BELMULLET*). Belmullet is one of the most remote towns in Ireland. Here distances are vast, as you will no doubt have discovered on the long drives from Mallaranny or Crossmolina. This is a landscape of bog, of mountains on the horizon, and of sandy beaches. Invariably you will have this nature all to yourself, for north-west Mayo – the region known as Erris – is one of the most sparsely inhabited corners of Ireland. Belmullet, home to around 1,000 people, is the biggest town. Situated in an Irish-speaking area, its name derives from the Irish for 'mouth of the Mullet peninsula', and it is located on the narrowest point of a long isthmus between Blacksod and Broadhaven bays.

However hard to imagine now, Belmullet could have been one of the great cities of Ireland. In the 1830s and in the 1910s, it was promoted as the ideal location for a great transatlantic port, connecting the 'old' and the 'new' worlds. Railways from London to Wales, and from Dublin to Belmullet would have brought thousands of passengers (and cargo) to steamships ready to make the big crossing to New York. As later with telegraphs, radio broadcasts, and aviation, the western coast of Ireland has long forged connections with North America.

In the end, the steamers went elsewhere. However, drawings survive showing the layout of the port town, and also the Grand Central-style railway station with shopping malls and fine dining for the journeys of the rich and famous. Belmullet is proud of this 'what if' aspect of its history, as you will find in the local museum and tourist office. The eagled-eyed might even notice that the road leading north out of the town is called, appropriately enough, 'American Street'.

IMAGES Opposite, top: Killala's medieval Round Tower.
Opposite, bottom: Aerial view of Dún Briste sea stack and Downpatrick Head.
Below: Blacksod Bay south of Belmullet.

It was the building of new roads through Erris in the 1810s and 1820s that spurred on the local landlord, William Henry Carter (1783–1859) to plan the new town of Belmullet (1824 is generally seen as its foundation date). Like Westport and Clifden, the town is formed of a geometrical plan of straight streets around a diamond. Caesar Otway, visiting in 1841, thought Belmullet the 'youngest town in Ireland'.

Today Belmullet is an important market centre with its own cultural scene. It is rapidly earning a strong reputation as a base for surfing, sailing and kayaking, as well as fishing. The Áras Inis Gluaire (Erris Arts Centre), hosts many exhibitions and concerts, and there is no shortage of things to see and do, especially in the summer months. The Féile Iorras arts festival, for example, takes place each July.

Whether you wish to explore the mainland of Erris or the peninsula, there is a huge amount to see and do on day trips from Belmullet, including:

Erris Head looped walk, a 10-minute drive. A marked walking trail at the northern tip of the Mullet peninsula, with plenty of crystal-clear water and interesting geology.

IMAGES Below: A rocky inlet near Erris Head.
Opposite, top: Hydrangeas overlooking the sandy beach at Portacloy.
Opposite, bottom: The lighthouse at Blacksod Point.

Blacksod Point lighthouse, a 20-minute drive. A sturdy lighthouse built in the 1860s at the southern point of the Mullet peninsula. When not windswept, this part of Mayo is a treasure-chest of sandy beaches and bathing spots.

Bangor Erris (*Beannchar*), a 20-minute drive. This small village of perhaps 300 people began as little more than a church and a police station. The region is well known for fishing on the mighty Owenmore River (*An Abhainn Mhór*, 'the big river'). There is excellent cycling in all directions, with the possibility of big loops via Crossmolina and Ballycastle.

Portacloy cliff walk and beach, a 30-minute drive. Whether you are interested in marked walking trails by cliffs or kayaking along the shores of a pristine, sandy beach, Portacloy will not disappoint.

The Céide Fields (*Achaidh Chéide*, 'flat-topped hill fields'), a 30-minute drive. Situated alongside cliffs, this is a historic site of international importance. You will find 6,000-year-old stone walls and the outline of dwellings, which were all rediscovered in the twentieth century. It is often cited as the most extensive Stone Age site of its kind in the world.

NEWPORT

NEWPORT (*BAILE UÍ FHIACHÁIN*). By Irish standards, Newport is a new town. Though its foundation dates back to 1720, almost all of what you see today is from the mid-Victorian era onwards. Indeed, when English tourists first reached here in the 1820s, they thought they had made it to the edge of the known world. William Hamilton Maxwell, whose tales of heroic adventures were published in 1832 as *Wild Sports of the West of Ireland*, commented that Newport was 'the last cluster of houses arrogating to itself the title of a town'; beyond was 'terra incognita'. There is still a small hint of that today, not least in the graceful red sandstone bridges that speak evocatively to its role in old coach-road and railway networks. From the higher and longer of the two – the seven-arched railway bridge (now a public promenade) that carried trains to Achill between the 1890s and the 1930s – Newport's place in the landscape of west Mayo becomes a little clearer. The town stands at the head of Clew Bay and the remarkable natural wonder of its hundreds of tiny islands.

Newport is one of Ireland's most monumental towns, best appreciated from the lay-by on the Westport side of the main road. Here the horizontal lines of the two bridges that span the *Abhainn na Daraí Duibhe* (the Black Oak River) are more than matched by the audacious tower of the town's Catholic church, built as recently as 1914–1918 in a muscular Hiberno-Romanesque architectural style by a man with a name to match: Rudolf Maximilian Butler of Dublin. Unfortunately, too many visitors rush through without stopping, for inside St Patrick's Church is one of the treasurers of the entire Wild Atlantic Way: the last window designed by the renowned artist Harry Clarke before his death in 1931 at the age of just forty-one. Appropriately named *The Last Judgement*, it is a tour-de-force example of a celebrated era of Irish art. Bring a good camera or even binoculars to appreciate fully the rich wall of vivid blues, greens, and purples. See if you can spot Clarke's self-portrait in the lower panels of the third window behind the altar – upside down beneath the devil, being forced into hell.

The town is compact and most of the activity happens within a few minutes' walk of the bridges. Look out for the best local food, drinks, and craft on Friday afternoons. In early August, the town comes alive with the Gráinne Uaile Festival to mark the life of Ireland's sixteenth-century 'pirate queen', Grace O'Malley. This is not to be missed, and there's even a pub with the same name for an outdoor pint in the evening sunshine.

Making Newport your base for a few days is highly recommended. There is much to do beyond the town, including:

The Westport–Achill Great Western Greenway, which passes through the town. Bicycle hire is available locally. If you would rather not cycle, there are opportunities for parking a car and walking at various intervals, including for example at Mallaranny, a 15-minute drive from Newport on the Achill road.

Burrishoole Friary, less than 5 minutes' drive. Situated by the sea, the extensive ruins of a Dominican friary founded around 1470 provide the perfect combination of architecture and landscape.

Letterkeen Loop Trailhead, a 20-minute drive. Trailhead 78 of the National Looped Walk network, this 12km walk takes you through forest and bog in the lower reaches of the Nephin Beg mountains. Beyond, as you will see marked on maps, is the vast expanse of Ballycroy National Park, established in 1998. Here you may have 15,000 hectares all to yourself in one of the largest expanses of peatland in Europe.

Clew Bay, accessible by various slipways and piers near the town. Kayaking, sightseeing trips and other water sport activity are available in the summer months. One of the many islands – Dorinish, a.k.a. 'Beatle Island' – was for several years the private escape of John Lennon.

Achill Island, a 30-minute drive. Accessible via a bridge, Achill is one of Ireland's most celebrated islands. Its northern and western edges are particularly mountainous and feature high sea cliffs. Head for Keem Bay where there is ample parking, and enjoy the Atlantic at its most dramatic.

IMAGES Top: The town of Newport with its two bridges.
Bottom left: The last stained-glass window by Harry Clarke can be seen in St Patrick's Church in Newport
Middle right: The former Westport-Achill railway is now a popular greenway.
Bottom right: Achill features spectacular sea cliffs comparable only to Sliabh Liag in Donegal.

WESTPORT

WESTPORT (*CATHAIR NA MART*, sometimes translated as 'stone fort of the cattle fair'). From its beginnings in the 1780s, Westport has been a little oasis of carefully planned urban life in the sparsely populated landscape of west Connacht. To the south are high mountains; to the north seemingly endless forestry and bog; and to the west the remarkable Clew Bay. Westport is an unusually well-organised town, a popular venue for the arts, and is often cited as the town with the best quality of life in Ireland. Now home to over 6,000 people, it has boomed in recent years with the building of the Great Western Greenway (see the chapter on Newport), the town's proximity to Ireland West (Knock) Airport, and its good train and road links to Dublin.

The name *Cathair na Mart* refers to an old and long-vanished village in what is now the grounds of Westport House. The Browne family, who until recent years still lived in the big house, cleared away this village in the 1780s and laid out a town with straight roads and a geometrical plan. Nowhere is their work better appreciated than on The Mall, a tree-lined promenade with several elegant bridges over the

Carrowbeg river. Few Irish towns have such a charming centre, so spending time in Westport is a must on any journey up or down the west coast. Amid the old Georgian buildings, there is no shortage of lovely cafés and wine bars. In St Mary's Catholic church, mostly built in the 1950s, you will find stained-glass windows that are a 'who's who' of twentieth-century Irish art, including important windows by George Walsh and Patrick Pye from the 1970s and 1980s.

The town is set a couple of kilometres back from the sea, which gives it more of the feel of an inland market town (comparable with Kilrush). In between is the 430-acre estate of Westport House, built by the aforementioned Brownes, the marquesses of Sligo. One of the great houses of the west of Ireland, it dates largely to the eighteenth century, and is the work of the prominent architects Richard Cassels and James Wyatt. In recent years, a local family has purchased the house; its gardens and looped walks are now free to visit, with a charge for tours inside the house (highly recommended).

As a cultural centre, Westport plays host to many festivals and events through the year. Many of these are staged at the Town Hall Theatre and sometimes in Westport House. For music lovers, the Folk and Bluegrass Festival happens each June, and the Festival of Chamber Music in September.

Beyond the town itself there is much to see and do, including:

Westport Quay, a 5-minute drive. The Great Western Greenway links the town with the quay and makes for a pleasant walk. Boat tours depart from the quay for Clew Bay.

Croagh Patrick (*Cruach Phádraig*, 'Patrick's mountain stack'), a 15-minute drive to the carpark at Murrisk. Croagh Patrick (764m) is a pilgrimage mountain and is known as 'Ireland's holy mountain', where St Patrick is said to have fasted for forty days. It rises steeply from the south shore of Clew Bay giving exceptional views from the summit. Each year on the last Sunday of July – known as Reek Sunday – pilgrims, often numbering over 20,000, take part in a climb up Casán Phádraig (Patrick's Path) to the summit; some follow the tradition of going barefoot as an act of penance.

IMAGES Opposite, top:The Carrowbeg river flows through Westport's elegant, tree-lined Mall.
Opposite, bottom: Croagh Patrick is a tough but rewarding hike.
Above: Westport House dates largely from the eighteenth century.

Castlebar (*Caisleán an Bharraigh*, 'Barry's Castle'), a 20-minute drive. The biggest town in Mayo (population 12,000 people), Castlebar played a prominent role in the 1798 rebellion.

National Museum of Ireland, Country Life, at Turlough Park, a 25-minute drive. The only branch of the National Museum of Ireland located outside of the capital, established in 2001. Free to visit.

Moore Hall, a 30-minute drive. Overlooking Lough Carra, this was the eighteenth-century home of the illustrious Moore family, including John Moore (1763–1799), President of the Government of the Province of Connacht at the time of the French invasion in 1798, and George Moore (1852–1933), the novelist. It is now an evocative ruin surrounded by woods.

CLIFDEN

CLIFDEN (*AN CLOCHÁN*, 'the stepping-stones'). Clifden is a classic, early nineteenth-century Irish 'frontier' town, built by the landlord John D'Arcy (1785–1839) from 1812 onwards. D'Arcy sought the help of the engineer Alexander Nimmo (see Spiddal, p.44), who planned the quay and the town's road link with Galway. Then, as now, Clifden's core is formed by the tight triangle of Market Street, Main Street, and Bridge Street. Hit hard during the Great Famine, it somehow clung on and developed as a tourist town in the late nineteenth century, especially after the railway arrived in 1895. Today it is home to around 1,600 people and is the gravitational centre for (and only town of any size in) the whole Connemara district of west Galway.

Clifden's streets are wide, and its shops are colourful. You never know who you will meet here: I have many fond memories during teenage visits of chatting with other hikers in Joyce's Clifden Town Hostel. People from all around the world are drawn here for all kinds of reasons, and some never leave. The English writer and cartographer Tim Robinson (1935–2020) lived for many years near Roundstone, from where he published his award-winning maps of Connemara, the Aran Islands, and the Burren. His two-volume Ruskinian masterpiece *Stones of Aran* and his *Setting Foot on the Shores of Connemara* are especially recommended for those interested in the deep human and natural history of the area.

The photographer's favourite view of Clifden is from the hill above Sky Road to the west, looking down on the town with the spires of its two parish churches framed by the Twelve Bens and other mountains in the distance. Perhaps John Alcock and Arthur Brown spotted the town in the distance at the end of their daring transatlantic voyage in June 1919, the first time anyone had made such a journey non-stop. Their Vickers Vimy landed hard into Deirgimleach Bog, about 6km south of Clifden, after a sixteen-hour journey from Newfoundland. Make sure to visit the monument there, along with the remains of the former Marconi Wireless Radio Station.

There are many festivals, cycles, runs, and other sporting events in Clifden throughout the year – one of the highlights is the annual Connemara Pony Show, held in late August.

Clifden is sometimes known as 'the capital of Connemara' because it forms the perfect base for day trips in every direction, including:

Sky Road and **Clifden Castle** (ruined), to the west of the town. Sky Road gives spectacular views of Clifden Bay. Look out for Clifden Castle, formerly John D'Arcy's home, built around 1818 in a fantasy Gothic style and which has been a ruin since the early 1900s. The walk to the Castle begins at a small carpark just off the road.

The Twelve Bens (*Na Beanna Beola*, 'the peaks of Beola'), a 15-minute drive. One of Connemara's great mountain ranges. The long hike across the south-facing Glencoaghan Horseshoe is recommended.

IMAGES Top left: The National Museum of Ireland, Country Life, is located at Turlough Park.
Top right: Ruins of Moore Hall, the eighteenth-century home of the Moore family.
Middle left: Clifden from the west, with the Twelve Bens in the background.
Middle right: The remains of Clifden Castle, formerly the home of John D'Arcy who built the town.
Bottom: Clifden Bay from Sky Road.

Cleggan and **Inisbofin**, a 15-minute drive. Ferries to *Inis Bó Finne* ('island of the white cow') depart from the small pier in Cleggan (journey time approximately 30 minutes). Bofin is home to around 180 people.

Letterfrack, **Diamond Hill**, and **Connemara National Park**, a 20-minute drive. Letterfrack (*Leitir Fraic*, 'the speckled hill') gives access to the western ranges of Connemara National Park. There are well-marked trails up Diamond Hill (442m), which gives panoramic views of the whole area.

Kylemore Abbey, a 25-minute drive. Formerly Kylemore Castle, a Victorian country house, and late a Benedictine convent. One of the most-visited sites in Connemara.

Roundstone (*Cloch na Rón*, 'seal's rock'), a 25-minute drive. This peaceful fishing village and the surrounding areas are home to a large artistic community. The bog road between Clifden and Roundstone makes for a great (and easy) cycle.

Dog's Bay and **Gurteen Bay**, a 30-minute drive. A tombolo with pristine beaches in every direction. Often cited as Ireland's finest bathing spot, with spectacular views of the mountains in the distance.

Killary Harbour, a 35-minute drive. This dramatic wind-swept fjord has Connacht's highest mountain, Mweelrea (*Cnoc Maol Réidh*, 'bald hill with the smooth top', 814m), on its northern shore.

KILRONAN, INISHMORE

CILL RÓNÁIN (*KILRONAN*), INIS MÓR (*INISHMORE*). I have never known a tourist to travel to the Aran Islands (*Oileáin Árann*) in search of an urban experience – and quite right too. Yet the islands more than deserve a place in this guide. Cill Rónáin village is about as big a settlement as you will find here, home to around 250 of the 850 people who live on Inis Mór (*Inishmore*), the largest of the three islands. The remarkable landscape of the Aran Islands is a continuation of the limestone pavements of the Burren in Clare, with countless clints (rocks) and grikes (cracks) that support many unusual plants including dwarf shrubs and orchids. Here, as on many of Ireland's islands, traditional customs and language survive stronger and more proudly than on the mainland. Around half of Inishmore's population speak the Irish language daily. Since the late nineteenth century, the Aran Islands have occupied a unique place in the Irish imagination as a bastion of indigenous culture, something explored in the playwright John Millington Synge's *The Aran Islands* (1907), and in countless films, novels and plays.

Inishmore (*Inis Mór*, 'big island'), as its name suggests, is a long ridge of an island: around 14km in length but only 2–3km in width. Most houses are towards the northern shore, on better land and away from the bare cliffs and raging seas. There are several ways to get to Cill Rónáin, and indeed to the other islands: by ferry from Ros an Mhíl (Rossaveal) in Galway or Doolin in Clare; or by a short flight from Connemara Airport. You will find plenty of accommodation options in and near the village, and horse-drawn carriage tours that will take you around the island. For many visitors, though, the favourite option is to rent a bicycle and enjoy the freedom of the quiet roads and the old-world charms of the thatched cottages and densely packed dry-stone walls. In Cill Rónáin you will find the Aran Sweater Market, selling jumpers known the world over. Nearby is the parish church, Seipéal Naomh Bríd agus Oilibhéir Pluincéid (the Church of Saints Brigid and Oliver Plunkett), built of rough limestone blocks in 1903–1905.

The Aran Islands are famed for their traditional music and dance and you will find both in abundance in the summer months. There is also a half-marathon on Inishmore in April, and for those who grew up watching the *Father Ted* sitcom, an annual 'Tedfest' in October (see also Inisheer/*Inis Oírr*, p.44). For those more interested in the natural world and ancient history, the southern coast of Inishmore is spectacularly rewarding. As you pass clusters of traditional cottages and small sandy beaches, the cliffs of the southern coast soon appear. Here you can see the remarkable Teampall Bheanáin (St Benen's Oratory), built in the eleventh century. Towards the western end of the island, make sure to visit Dún Aonghasa, one of the finest prehistoric (c.1100BC) monuments in Europe, perched ominously atop 100-metre cliffs. Maybe someday a bad storm will take it all away! On your way there is *Poll na bPéist* (the 'hole of worms'), a giant rectangular pool where cliff divers sometimes compete. The rocks nearby give mesmerising views of the ocean but the giant swells can be extremely dangerous.

IMAGES Top: Boats at the pier of the peaceful fishing village of Roundstone.
Bottom left: The dramatic fjord at Killary Harbour.
Bottom right: Aerial view of Dún Aonghusa fort on Inishmore's cliffs.

Beyond Inishmore, if you have the time, you can explore the other islands:

Inis Meáin (*Inishmaan*), the middle island, just 5km by 2km. The least affected by modern mass tourism, and home now to around 180 people. As on the other Aran Islands, the ferry landing spot and airfield are on the northern shore. Inishmaan's maze of dry-stone walls is a sight to behold. Look out for Teach Synge (Synge's cottage), where the playwright holidayed in 1898–1902, and which is now a museum.

Inis Oírr (*Inisheer*), the easternmost island, closest to Clare, and 3km by 3km in size. This is a popular tourist destination owing to its proximity to Doolin, and is home to around 260 people. In a winter storm in 1960, the 50m ship *MV Plassy* was wrecked on the island's eastern shore. Now a great rusting hulk, it was made famous by its appearance on the fictional 'Craggy Island' in the opening credits of *Father Ted*.

SPIDDAL

AN SPIDÉAL (*SPIDDAL*). There are two ways of getting from Galway to Connemara (Conamara): the main road, inland, through Oughterard, and the coast road via Spiddal. In between is a great expanse of water, bog, and mountains. Both routes are hugely rewarding but, if you have the time, the coast road is the one to go for. An Spidéal (Spiddal) is home to around 250 people; it derives its name from the Irish for a hospital – *ospidéal* – though whatever was there before is long gone!

Spiddal is at the outer edge of the Galway commuting belt and still retains many of its old-world charms. On a warm spring day, the village is pure heaven – a welcome break from the crowds and traffic in the city. Here the sun glistens across Galway Bay with the Burren in the distance, and the sand is soft on your feet. Many small fishing boats find shelter behind the two stone piers, one on either side of the river (the *Abhainn Bhoth Loiscthe*) that divides the village. Alexander Nimmo (1783–1832), the great Scottish engineer, built the smaller of these piers (known as *An tSeancéibh*, the 'old pier') in the 1820s. Nearby is the remarkable little Hiberno-Romanesque style church of St Enda, built in 1904–1907 by the architect William Scott. It speaks to the revival of all things 'Irish' from the late nineteenth century onwards: language, crafts, clothing, sports, and architecture. I have long held this church in special regard on account of its many connections with the Killanin family, who lived in the village. Michael Morris (1914–1999), the 3rd Lord Killanin, along with the archaeologist Michael Duignan, wrote what is arguably the best Irish guidebook ever published: *The Shell Guide to Ireland* (1962, 1967), which has had a major influence on the writing of this book. Inside St Enda's Church, look out for the early twentieth-century stained-glass windows by Sarah Purser (1848–1943) and also a window dedicated to Morris.

In the summer months, Spiddal is busy with Irish-language students, mostly from the cities but also a sizeable number from the United States. The pubs are filled with music: An Droighneán Donn, near the church, is especially recommended (their advertisement says it all: 'Bia, Ól agus Ceol' – 'food, drink and music'). In July, the village hosts the Féile Traidphicnic, a family and community festival of music and art.

Beyond Spiddal, there is a huge tract of countryside to explore, including:

Bearna (*Barna*) and Silverstrand beach, a 10-minute drive. Bearna is now home to over 2,000 people and is at ever-increasing risk of being swallowed up by the suburbs of Galway city. Nearby is the beautiful Silverstrand beach, with plenty of parking, walking routes, and small cliffs – often very busy in the summer months.

Uachtar Ard (*Oughterard*) and Aughnanure Castle, a 30-minute drive. Oughterard (population around 1,400) is one of the few towns on the 80km road between Galway and Clifden. It is a useful place to get provisions before heading out fishing, kayaking, or hiking. About 4km away, near the shores of Lough Corrib, is the fantastic sixteenth-century Aughnanure Castle, which welcomes visitors. Built by the O'Flaherty family, its mean-looking tower and surrounding walls survive in excellent condition.

IMAGES Below, top: Fields and dry-stone walls on Inis Meáin.
Below, middle: Shipwreck *MV Plassy* on the stony beach at Inis Oírr.
Bottom left: Low tide at Spiddal's harbour.
Right: Stained-glass window in St Enda's Church in Spiddal, commemorating Michael Morris (1914–1999), the 3rd Lord Killanin.

Lough Corrib, close to Oughterard. The second largest lake in Ireland (176km^2), it is studded with hundreds of islands, and is a favourite spot for fishing and cruises.

Maam Cross and the **Maumturk Mountains**, a 40-minute drive. This is a landscape of bare rocky mountains rising straight out of endless bog (and so very different from Cork or Kerry). Maam Cross is a convenient spot (with a large hotel/pub) from which to start a day out in what is known as 'Joyce Country'. A cycle to An Mám (*Maum*) and onwards to An Líonán (*Leenaun*), returning via the R344, is highly recommended (and challenging).

Cuan Chasla (*Cashla Bay*), **Cuan an Fhir Mhóir** (*Greatman's Bay*), and **Cuan Chill Chiaráin** (*Kilkieran Bay*), all within 25–45 minutes of An Spidéal. This is a complex landscape of islands, causeways, pristine white beaches and vast expanses of bog. Near Rosmuc (*Rosmuck*) is the cottage once owned by the revolutionary Patrick Pearse, now a museum (Ionad Cultúrtha an Phiarsaigh).

IMAGES Top: Patrick Pearse's cottage, Rosmuc.
Bottom: The bare mountains between Maam Cross and Leenaun in Connemara.

Galway
Kilronan
Kinvara
Lahinch
Kilkee
Kilrush
Ballybunion

GALWAY TO THE SHANNON ESTUARY

Evening at the Cliffs of Moher.

GALWAY

GALWAY (*GAILLIMH*). Galway is the largest city or town on the Wild Atlantic Way route and is now home to more than 80,000 people. A phenomenally successful and wealthy place, known around the world for its culture and history, it is also a gateway to west Connacht. Most tourists make it their business to spend at least a few days here, and thousands of exchange students visit each year, many taking courses at the National University of Ireland, Galway (NUIG) – now home to a community of almost 20,000 staff and students.

The locals call themselves Galwegians or Tribesmen, and they are in general very proud of their city and its long history. The most common complaints will, invariably, be the constant traffic jams and the fact that it rains, on average, every second day. Galway is Ireland's wettest city, but after some time living there, I found that I got very used to it, and as the old saying goes, 'there's no such thing as bad weather, only unsuitable clothing'.

Galway is best explored on foot. It often appears more like a huge, overgrown town than a city and most visitors from the continent will immediately notice the lack of high-rise buildings or what feel like 'urban' neighbourhoods. It is only here and there that it feels like a city: around Eyre Square, near the Cathedral (just maybe), and on the American-style one-way roads that run in straight lines near the docks and marina. A little further out, you will see mostly one- or two-storey houses like the edge of any small Irish town. Galway has in some ways outgrown itself with its own success, and much of the local politics now centres on whether it is seen as a big town or as a small city – you can decide for yourself!

Galway's exponential growth stands in contrast to the many disasters that befell it in times long past. A fort on the river dating back to the early twelfth century developed into an Anglo-Norman town that was awarded a charter in 1484. Loyal to the English crown but geographically remote, Galway did its own thing – trading with France, Spain, and Scandinavia. The exchange with Spain, in particular, is still seen as a way of explaining the distinctive darker features of some Galway people ('her hair was black and her eyes were blue', as the song 'Galway Girl' goes – something you're bound to hear at least once during any visit). Long ago, the town was ruled by fourteen merchant families – known as the 'Tribes of Galway', hence the name 'Tribesmen' today. Their prosperous little walled town suffered hugely in the Cromwellian era (with a nine-month blockade ending in surrender), in the Williamite wars (when they supported the losing side), and during the Great Famine. The town's long decline continued until the early twentieth century when the population stood at little over 13,000; by the 1960s, it had grown to 25,000; by the 1990s it was over 50,000; and now, as mentioned above, it is around 80,000.

For all of its growing pains, Galway is extremely fortunate to have such a wonderful natural landscape. It is divided in two by a river (*Abhainn na Gaillimhe*) that comes crashing through the centre of the city, taking an average of 100 tons of water per second on the short journey from the vast Lough Corrib to the sea. Look out for the white-water kayakers and the fishermen who know this river and its tricks so well. In the winter, especially after heavy rain, I have stood on the boardwalk near O'Brien's Bridge and wondered how the bridge wasn't simply washed away with all the water coming at it so violently. No other river in Ireland but the Shannon has such a flow.

From this bridge, a looped walk is highly recommended. Heading upriver towards the Salmon Weir Bridge, you will see the dome of the gigantic Catholic cathedral, finished as late as 1965. Inside, in the Mortuary Chapel, there are mosaics (by Patrick Pollen) that commemorate the revolutionary Patrick Pearse alongside (strange as it may seem) the American president John F. Kennedy, who visited Galway soon before his assassination in 1963. Crossing the bridge, you will enter a small square with the city's courthouse on one side and the Town Hall Theatre on the other. In times past, a British royal arms sat atop this courthouse; after independence, it was removed, but somehow survived and can now be found hidden around the back of the old quadrangle of NUIG. Walking south towards Eglinton Street brings you to Eyre Square, the centre of the city. Between here and O'Brien's Bridge is the historic core – Shop Street, High Street, Middle Street – where Galway's nightlife happens. Amid the crowds on Shop Street, look out for Lynch's Castle (now a bank), a richly decorated sixteenth-century tower house. Nearby is the Church of Ireland Church of St Nicholas, filled with many interesting monuments dating back to medieval times.

IMAGES Top: Galway's imposing Catholic cathedral was built in the 1960s on the site of a former jail.
Bottom left: The river comes crashing through the centre of the city.
Bottom right: The National University of Ireland, Galway (NUIG).

If you want to explore more, walk downriver from O'Brien's Bridge to the Spanish Arch, where crowds gather by the water on summer evenings. Nearby are the city museum and various galleries, and the 'Long Walk', as it is called, that takes you down to the docks. On the opposite side of the river, you will see traditional sailing boats tied up in the Eglinton Basin. Here there are many wonderful pubs, restaurants, and late-night cafés on Dominick Street and William Street. The housing estates nearby are known as the Claddagh – formerly an Irish-speaking fishing town of thatched cottages (cleared in the 1930s). Further west is Salthill, a favourite spot for summer holiday vacations, with beaches and an old diving tower that is one of Galway's most photographed landmarks.

While most towns on Ireland's Wild Atlantic Way have one or two festivals a year, Galway exists in a state of almost permanent festivities, too numerous to list, as you will discover when you get there. For those seeking solitude, a walk along the Eglinton Canal and into the NUIG campus is highly recommended. It is a full 4km from the sea to the viewing point for the ruined, ivy-clad Menlo Castle, and from where the city feels surprisingly distant.

KINVARA AND SOUTH GALWAY BAY

You may be surprised to find a section on the southern side of Galway Bay in a book dedicated to Ireland's Wild Atlantic towns. While there are *some* towns along the way, it is fair to say that this is a part of Ireland – with a countryside that is mesmerisingly beautiful, bleak, and empty – best known for its distinctive Burren landscape. Kinvara is about as big as towns get on this coastline, but with a population of less than 1,500 people, many foreigners would probably think of it more as a village.

Stretching from Doolin to Crusheen and from Kinvara to the appropriately named Black Head is the vast expanse of the Burren (*Boirinn*, 'rocky ground'), a glaciated karst landscape. Here rivers vanish into the ground only to re-emerge several kilometres further on, and exotic flora and fauna eek out an existence in the many cracks of the limestone pavements. There is something otherworldly about the scale of the Burren, and it is now rightly a natural environment protected and studied by scientists from far and near. In the 1650s, one of Oliver Cromwell's soldiers is reported to have said that it was a countryside 'where there is not water enough to drown a man, wood enough to hang one nor earth enough to bury one'. Some of the best hiking routes can be found in the 1,500-hectare Burren National Park, about 8km north of the village of Corrofin (or a 30-minute drive from Kinvara). For those who grew up watching British and Irish television, 'Fr Ted's house' is nearby, and it is possible to book a tour. Other popular Burren walks can be found near the village of Ballyvaughan, and at Black Head, where on a fine day you might spot in the distance both Galway and the Aran Islands. Local detailed maps for walking are available throughout the area.

KINVARA (*CINN MHARA*, 'head of the sea' – the same, then, as Kenmare, Co. Kerry). Kinvara is an oasis of greenery after a day in the Burren. Situated at the head of a small bay, it is an old fishing village that now attracts many tourists and even some commuters to Galway. There are many pubs and restaurants on Main Street and near the pier – Fox's wine bar and pizzeria is especially recommended. Kinvara hosts an Irish music festival in May (*Fleadh na gCuach*, 'the cuckoo festival') and a regatta in August (*Cruinniú na mBád*, 'gathering of boats'), where you can see red-sailed Galway hookers, the bay's traditional fishing boats.

Beyond exploring the Burren there is much to see and do near Kinvara, including:

Dunguaire Castle (*Caisleán Dhún Guaire*), at the eastern edge of the village. This sixteenth-century tower house of the O'Hynes family, with a six-sided bawn (surrounding wall), is perhaps the most picture-perfect castle in Ireland. Now comprehensively restored, it is welcoming to those interested in learning about Irish history and culture.

Ballyvaughan (*Baile Uí Bheacháin*, 'Ó Beachán's town'), a 20-minute drive. At the head of another small bay, Ballyvaughan is the perfect Burren base. Aillwee Cave, a fascinating limestone underworld, is a 5-minute drive south of the village.

IMAGES Top left: Plants growing through cracks in the bedrock in the Burren.
Top right: Dunguaire Castle, Kinvara.
Bottom left: Fishing boats at the Claddagh.
Bottom right: The bustling pedestrianised city centre on a summer's day.

Gort (*An Gort*), a 20-minute drive inland. An unusually cosmopolitan inland town, this home to 3,000 people was recently linked to Limerick and Galway by a motorway. The Gallery Café on the market square is more than enough of a reason to visit. Gort and the surrounding landscape are strongly associated with the poet William Butler Yeats (1865–1939): within a 10-minute drive of the town you will find Coole Park, now a 400-hectare nature reserve, and 'Thoor Ballylee', a riverside tower house where the poet lived in the 1920s.

The Slieve Aughty (*Sliabh Eachtaí*) **hills**, a 30-minute drive inland. If the coast is busy with tourists, take your bicycle to Derrybrien and head for Woodford, returning via Caher. You will have it all to yourself.

Loughrea (*Baile Locha Riach*, 'town of the grey lake'), a 35-minute drive inland. St Brendan's Cathedral (built 1897–1903) has the single most important collection of twentieth-century Irish stained glass of any building in the world, with windows by A.E. Child, Sarah Purser, Michael Healy, Evie Hone, and Patrick Pye.

LAHINCH AND WEST CLARE

LAHINCH (*LEACHT UÍ CHONCHUBHAIR*). County Clare is situated in Munster but around Lahinch the landscape feels much more like Connacht. As the sailing guidebook warns, there are 'few harbours, and no good ones' on Clare's coastline. Instead, you will find spectacular cliffs, sandy beaches, and big rolling waves. Nowhere is this truer than in Lahinch, where the winter storms smash walls of water against the village's pubs and shops. Unlike Kilkee, there is nothing to stop the big swells on their way in – but this also makes Lahinch a favourite for surfers. It is home to around 650 people in the winter, but easily triple that in the summer.

The village's name comes from an anglicised version of *Leath Inse*, 'peninsula', referring to the fact that the village is wedged between the Inagh river and the sea. Its proper name in Irish is *Leacht Uí Chonchubhair*, 'the memorial cairn of O'Connor'. Lahinch developed in the late nineteenth century as a seaside bathing resort but there are several traces of its earlier history that have survived, including large earthen ringforts that are visible from the main road to Ennistymon (to your left-hand side as you leave the village). A few kilometres north, near the bridge over the Inagh river, you can see the gaunt ruins of Dough Castle. The castle is situated within the grounds of the Lahinch Golf Club, founded in the 1890s, and today a very popular links course, sometimes hosting major international competitions.

Main Street wisely has its back to the sea, and this is where all the best pubs and restaurants are to be found. The street is marked at one end by the tower of the parish church, built by the renowned Derry architect Liam McCormick in the early 1950s. After a day on the beach, head to Kenny's Bar for live music on weekend nights year-round and more often during the summer. You will soon forget that the ocean is close by, but no doubt you will be reminded where you are at the end of the night when you turn the corner on Main Street and hear the waves once more. That's a classic Lahinch experience for me.

Interesting places to visit beyond Lahinch include:

Ennistymon (or Ennistimon, *Inis Díomáin*), a 5-minute drive (4km), with an excellent cycle path all the way. Lahinch's big brother, Ennistymon is home to around 1,100 people and is built where the Inagh river cascades spectacularly over great slabs of rock. You can get up close to the falls by walking through the stone arch next to Byrne's. At the Lahinch end of the town there is another Liam McCormick church, built again in the 1950s and a big influence on Irish architects of that era.

IMAGES Left: W.B. Yeats's former home at Ballylee.
Below: The County Clare coastline is renowned for its big waves.
Bottom: The Inagh river makes a dramatic appearance in the centre of Ennistymon.

Cliffs of Moher, a 15-minute drive. The chances are that if you are visiting Ireland, you will already know exactly why this is such a classic stopping-off point on the Wild Atlantic Way – 14km of walking trails from near Liscannor to Doolin, with 200-metre cliffs straight down to the ocean. Boat tours take you up close to the cliffs and the many birds, dolphins and seals that visit the area.

Doolin (*Dúlainn*), a 20-minute drive. Famed for its traditional Irish music, Doolin is also home to extensive limestone caves that can be visited (4km north of the village). Ferries to the Aran Islands (see the chapter on Kilronan) leave from Doolin pier.

Lisdoonvarna (*Lios Dúin Bhearna*, 'fort of the gapped keep'), a 20-minute drive. A small town known for its large Matchmaking Festival each September, one of the biggest events of its kind in Europe.

Ennis (*Inis*, 'island'), a 30-minute drive. The largest town in County Clare, home to more than 25,000 people. Ennis has all the amenities of a county town, including trains to Galway, Limerick, and Dublin. For old-world charm, head to Abbey St. and its many lanes. Nearby a large monument celebrates Daniel O'Connell's election as a member of parliament in 1828, an event that resulted in Catholic Emancipation the following year (see the chapter on Sneem). A town best experienced on foot.

KILRUSH AND KILKEE

KILRUSH (*CILL ROIS*, 'the church of the woods'). Kilrush is unusual in being tucked away from the Wild Atlantic by the Loop Head peninsula. Yet beyond the call of seabirds, Kilrush has the feel of an old inland market town. It grew rapidly in the boom years of the Napoleonic Wars (around 1800) with exports of agricultural produce and light industry, spurred on by the local magnate, John Ormsby Vandeleur (1765–1828), whose family had Dutch ancestors. Vandeleur created impressively wide new streets such as Frances Street (heading down to the marina), and a proper town centre – the Market Square – with lots of high-quality Georgian architecture to match. Tourists often find Ireland's narrow streets and roads anxiety-inducing but Kilrush is quite the exception! In early August, the town hosts the Kilrush Traditional Music and Set Dancing Festival.

By the 1840s, the town had swelled to almost 5,000 people but there was a darker side to the Vandeleurs that locals will be only too keen to tell you about: during the Great Famine, they were notorious for their harsh treatment of their tenants, and by the 1880s their evictions of the rural poor brought them international reproach. The town fell into a long decline, and even today the population is only half what it was back then. But, in an admirable way, the town appears to have reconciled itself with its past, both at the Museum of Irish Rural Life in the town centre, and at the beautiful Vandeleur Walled Garden and Woodland Bistro, 1km southeast of the town centre on a safe footpath. The Walled Garden, adjacent to the now-vanished 'big house', opened in the late 1990s and is free to visit. There are paths that lead into a large expanse of forestry, where a 5km park run is staged on Saturday mornings.

KILKEE (*CILL CHAOI*, 'the church of Caoi'). Near to Kilrush is its smaller sister, Kilkee, once connected by a narrow-gauge railway that ran from Ennis to West Clare. Kilkee, now home to around 1,000 people, began as a fishing village and developed into a seaside resort of considerable fame in the nineteenth century. Its long sandy beach at the head of the horseshoe-shaped Moore Bay is partially sheltered by reefs – and there are interesting rock pools nearby. If in search of food and drink, head to the lively O'Curry Street, where you will find lots of outdoor seating in the summer months.

Beyond Kilrush and Kilkee, there is much to see and do (with driving times here broadly similar for departures from either town):

Inis Cathaigh ('the island of Cathaigh', also known as Scattery Island). A short ferry trip from Kilrush marina. One of the largest islands in the Shannon estuary, Inis Cathaigh is awash with history, from monastic ruins and a round tower to a Napoleonic-era artillery battery. The island has been uninhabited since the 1970s. There is a local tradition that pebbles from the island are believed to protect sailors from shipwreck.

IMAGES Top: The centre of Ennis is made up of old narrow winding streets.
Middle left: Kilkee's sandy beach at the head of Moore Bay.
Bottom left: Round tower on Inis Cathaigh/Scattery Island.
Bottom right: Sculpture of dolphins at Kilrush marina.

Carrigaholt (*Carraig an Chabhaltaigh*), a 20-minute drive. *Carraig an Chabhaltaigh*, the 'rock of the fleet', is an apporpriate name for a bay where, in 1588, Spanish Armada ships took refuge during a storm. The large castle was built by the McMahons in the 1480s. Dolphin-watching tours depart from the pier.

Quilty (*Coillte*, 'woods'), a 25-minute drive. Where the woods of its name used to be is now a small fishing village. In 1907, the French ship *Leon XIII* was wrecked nearby, but its crew were rescued by heroic local fishermen. The ship's bell now stands in front of the altar in the Catholic church, which is dedicated to Our Lady, Star of the Sea. The dramatic rescue is commemorated in a stained-glass window. The village's Leon XIII festival involves, appropriately enough, currach racing (commemorating the little boats the fishermen used for the rescue).

Loop Head Lighthouse, a 40-minute drive. At the end of a narrow peninsula, the lighthouse was built in the 1840s. A large World War II-era 'Éire' sign stands nearby. A place to watch the sun go down.

BALLYBUNION

BALLYBUNION (*BAILE AN BHUINNEÁNAIGH*).
In the middle stretches of the Wild Atlantic Way – approximately between Connemara and Tralee – the coastline is typically sandier and more suited to swimming and surfing than further south on the jagged Kerry and Cork peninsulas. Ballybunion (*Baile an Bhuinneánaigh*, simply 'the town of Bunnion') is one of these classic big-beach seaside towns, and people have been coming here since the early nineteenth century to admire the rolling waves, the eaten-away cliffs, and the many dramatic sea arches and caves. All the best pubs and restaurants are to be found on Main Street as it makes its way gently down to the sea. Much of the town is made up of sizable colonies of holiday homes for the summer residents who more than double the permanent population of just under 2,000 people.

Standing proudly in the centre of the main beach, atop a rocky outcrop, are the ruins of Ballybunion Castle, built in the thirteenth century but mostly destroyed three hundred years later in the wars that wreaked havoc on so much of Munster. Little is now left except one of the walls, pierced by narrow slit windows that capture the rays of the setting sun. The Castle serves as a useful navigation aid for walks along the beaches and is visible for many kilometres around.

The beaches are known locally as the men's, ladies', and nun's, though you will be glad to hear that no segregation is imposed! To the north of the town centre, around nun's beach, there are breathtaking cliff walks, sea arches and caves. Further south, the long sandy beach runs parallel to the world-renowned Ballybunion Golf Course, founded in 1893, and now home to two links golf courses that attract many elite golfers. A statue of Bill Clinton marks his regular visits to the course.

When the barometric pressure is low, there are many warm pubs to enjoy, old-fashioned amusement arcades for the kids, and, at the eastern end of the town centre, the Tinteán Theatre, which puts on shows, concerts and stand-up comedy through the tourist season.

Apart from Ballybunion's celebrated beaches, north County Kerry and parts of west Limerick are definitely off the beaten track for tourist traffic. This only makes them all the more enjoyable to explore, and there are many curious and interesting options for daytrips, including:

Knockanore Hill, less than a 10-minute drive. It is possible to drive all the way to the TV masts and aerials on top, but the full loop from Ballybunion is just over 12km on foot. From Knockanore there are majestic views of the coastline from Kerry Head to Loop Head and the lower reaches of the Shannon estuary.

IMAGES Top left: Carrigaholt Castle, visible for many kilometres around.
Top right: Loop Head Lighthouse is situated at the southwestern tip of County Clare.
Middle right: The world-renowned Ballybunion Golf Course at sunset.
Bottom: The ruins of Ballybunion Castle serve as a navigational aid for walks along the sandy beaches.

Lartigue Monorail and **Museum**, a 15-minute drive (to Listowel). Between 1888 and 1924, a highly unusual (and impractical!) monorail steam train ran between Ballybunion and Listowel. Designed by the French engineer Charles Lartigue, it mostly served to bring holidaymakers to the sea before the era of motorcars. A replica train along with 1km of track has been recreated at this visitor attraction in Listowel, set up by local volunteers around twenty years ago. A true 'hidden gem'.

Tarbert Bridewell, a 25-minute drive. Tarbert is on the Wild Atlantic Way route and has a ferry that crosses the Shannon to County Clare. In the centre of the village, you will find a mean-looking bridewell prison, built in the 1830s by a Mr Pain from England. Restored in recent years, it now welcomes visitors.

Great Southern Trail Greenway, a 30-minute drive (to Abbeyfeale). More than 40km of former railway is now a walking and cycling route, connecting Rathkeale, Newcastle West, and Abbeyfeale. The route is not without some hills and there is a short tunnel at Barnagh near Newcastle West.

Foynes Flying Boat & Maritime Museum, a 40-minute drive. Foynes port is also a Wild Atlantic Way destination and is home to a remarkable maritime museum that explores early transatlantic aviation. The museum boasts the world's only full-size replica of a Boeing 314 Clipper, commemorating *The Yankee Clipper* that refuelled at Foynes in the 1930s while on long journeys from England to Canada and the USA.

IMAGES Below: Tarbert Bridewell was built in the 1830s and is now a museum.
Opposite, top: Tunnel on the Great Southern Trail Greenway.
Opposite, bottom: The port of Foynes.

ARKLOW FOREST

Tralee
Dingle
Killorglin
Cahersiveen
Sneem
Kenmare
Glengarriff
Allihies
Castletownbere

TRALEE TO GLENGARRIFF

Garnish Island with Glengarriff Bay in the distance.

IMAGES Top left: Tralee Courthouse, designed by William Vitruvius Morrison in the 1820s.
Top right: The well-preserved ruins of Ardfert Cathedral.
Bottom: Picturesque Blennerville with its elegant windmill.

TRALEE

TRALEE (*TRÁ LÍ*, the 'strand of the River Lee'). Most of the towns on Ireland's Wild Atlantic Way are relatively small. Tralee is different: it feels properly urban, with a long and proud history as the county town of Kerry, and it has Georgian streetscapes to match. When I visited as a child from rural West Cork, Tralee struck me as almost metropolitan with its big buildings and that classic trio of any 'big town' in Ireland: roundabouts, having to pay for parking, and the option of a good Chinese restaurant. Now home to 24,000 people, Tralee is the largest town in Kerry (despite Killarney's pretensions) and the second largest urban centre on the entire Wild Atlantic Way, after Galway city. New apartment blocks in the vicinity of the train station – mostly student accommodation for Munster Technological University – give the town an appearance strikingly different from the usual branding of a Kerry town. Though it is 'talked down' by some Irish people, there is a huge amount to see and do in Tralee and the surrounding countryside.

Trá Lí, the 'strand of the River Lee', has been around for the best part of 800 years. The Dominicans had a friary here in the 1240s, and much later the earls of Desmond built their main castle in the town. After the upheavals of the fifteenth century, Tralee ended up in the hands of the English soldier and general chancer, Sir Edward Denny (1547–1600), whose descendants did much to improve the town. In the 1820s, they laid out Denny Street – arguably the finest street in Kerry – and a few years later oversaw the building of one of Ireland's best courthouses, designed by a gifted architect with a name to match: William Vitruvius Morrison (1794–1838). Both are worth a visit: at the southern end of Denny Street is the large tree-lined Town Park and the Kerry County Museum, occupying a grand civic building erected in the 1920s. And on the plinth of the courthouse, you will find two large commemorative cannons, in memory of those Kerrymen who fought for empire in the Crimean war and the Indian rebellion (both in the 1850s). By contrast, the Kerrymen who fought *against* empire are celebrated nearby at the large Pikeman Statue (1905), though the sculpture you see today is a 1930s replacement of one that the Black and Tans hacked apart during the War of Independence. These complexities of Irish history are best mediated with a pint at the adjacent Pikeman Bar.

Tralee is a well-connected and outward-looking place: Kerry's international airport is just fifteen minutes away, and there is a good train service to Dublin, along with ever-improving roads. The town is best known for its annual Rose of Tralee Festival in August, a going concern since 1959. A distinctly Irish take on the American beauty pageant, the Rose of Tralee is an overwhelming international roller-coaster that brings a buzz to the town unlike any other festival in Ireland. If you happen to be in Tralee when it's happening, you will never forget it. For millions of Irish people at home and abroad, it's a two-night guilty-pleasure TV show that they will likely deny watching.

Beyond the town centre, there are many options for day trips:

Blennerville, a 45-minute walk. Located a few kilometres downstream of Tralee, Blennerville is best known for its elegant windmill, built in 1800 and one of the tallest in Ireland at 21m. Restored in the early 1990s, it is now a visitor attraction. The best way to get there is to walk along the towpath of the former Tralee Ship Canal, built between 1832 and 1846.

Ardfert Cathedral, a 10-minute drive. The well-preserved ruins of a muscular medieval cathedral dating back to the Romanesque period are dramatically sited in the centre of a village. Ardfert has many associations with St Brendan the Navigator, who reputedly sailed all the way across the Atlantic in the sixth century.

Banna Strand, a 15-minute drive. One of north Kerry's classic long sandy beaches. The prominent nationalist Roger Casement (1864–1916) was arrested here on attempting to land weapons from a German U-Boat in advance of the Easter Rising. Convicted of treason, he was hanged at Pentonville Prison in London in August 1916.

DINGLE

DINGLE (*DAINGEAN UÍ CHÚIS*). At 10°16′ west, Dingle is the most westerly town of any size on the island of Ireland – making it the perfect place to enjoy a long summer evening and watch the sun set at just past 10pm. Properly called *Daingean Uí Chúis* ('the fort of Ó Cúis') because of its location within the *Corca Duibhne* Gaeltacht, Dingle is a proud, bustling town that looms large in the Irish imagination of the western seaboard. Home to around 2,000 people, it is surrounded by spectacular mountains, steep and narrow roads, sandy beaches, and remote – now uninhabited – islands. It feels like a distilled, concentrated version of the entire Wild Atlantic Way.

Dingle is situated in a sheltered bay and serves as a busy port for the landing of fish. It traces its origins to the Norman period, and by the sixteenth century a large proportion of the wine imported into Ireland from France and Spain landed here. Returning Spanish vessels sometimes brought pilgrims to the shrine of St James at Santiago de Compostela, a connection which lives on today in the small Church of Ireland parish church in the centre of the town, rebuilt around 1810 and dedicated to St James. The town's fortune collapsed in the wars and rebellions around the year 1700, recovered somewhat with the linen trade in the eighteenth century, but then suffered enormously during the Great Famine of 1845–1852, with the population today roughly half what it was before this watershed event. Dingle's more recent history has been dominated by fishing and then the development of tourism.

Many of Dingle's excellent pubs and restaurants are located on Main Street, Green Street, and by the waterfront, while B&Bs, hostels and hotels are to be found on The Mall and at the outer approaches to the town. If possible, park near the edge or by the marina (for a modest charge) and explore the town on foot, which will allow you to escape the vagaries of the one-way streets. This is especially advised during the many festivals for which Dingle is known – Féile Na Bealtaine at the beginning of May, the horse races in August, and the Food Festival in early October, to name but a few. Parties in Dingle, especially for the soon-to-be-married, are known to go on late into the night!

From the marina there are multiple boat tours that explore the wildlife of Dingle Bay, the cliffs and the Blaskets (for which boats also depart from Ventry and Dunquin further west). The Blaskets (*Na Blascaodaí*) are a sight to behold when the weather is right; the last residents of these Irish-speaking islands were removed to the mainland in the 1950s. Generations of Irish schoolchildren learned about the Blaskets through the work of Tomás Ó Criomhthain (1856–1937) and Peig Sayers (1873–1958), and you can experience their world by hiking amidst the ruined cottages on the steep slopes of Great Blasket Island, 6km from end to end. In good visibility you will be able to see beyond the inhospitable reaches of Inishtooskert, Tearaght, Inishnabro, and Inishvickillane (purchased by an Irish taoiseach – prime minister – in the 1980s).

For those less enthusiastic for Atlantic swells, there is no shortage of excellent daytrips, including:

The Conor Pass (*An Chonair*), a 10-minute drive. One of the highest mountain passes in Ireland at 456m, the Conor Pass is a well-known cycling challenge.

Ventry (*Ceann Trá*), a 15-minute drive. Much quieter than Dingle, Ventry is home to a wonderful sandy beach.

Gallarus Oratory (*Séipéilín Ghallarais*), a 15-minute drive. An ancient church built with tightly bound stones, Gallarus Oratory gives the appearance of an upturned boat. It is accessible to the public, with parking available nearby. The beautiful Wine Strand is a short walk away.

Brandon Mountain (*Cnoc Bréanainn*), a 20-minute drive. One of the highest peaks in Ireland at 952m, and a bigger climb than Carrauntoohil owing to the sea-level start, Brandon forms part of a pilgrimage route (the 'Kerry Camino'), with parking available off the R549 road to the southwest of the peak (and elsewhere). In perfect visibility, Brandon's dramatic ridge has been spotted from Dog's Bay in Connemara, 130km away.

Castlegregory (*Caisleán Ghriaire*), a 30-minute drive. This cosy little village gives access to vast sandy beaches and the Magharee Islands.

IMAGES Top: The bustling town of Dingle serves as a busy port for fishing boats.
Middle left: Ruined cottages on Great Blasket Island.
Bottom left: Aerial view of the Conor Pass, one of Ireland's highest mountain passes.
Bottom: Gallarus Oratory, an early Christian church built with tightly bound stones.

KILLORGLIN

KILLORGLIN (*CILL ORGLAN*, 'Orglan's church'). For too many visitors to Kerry, Killorglin is simply the crossing of a river on the drive from Killarney to the ends of the Iveragh peninsula. This is a shame, as it's a perfect place to base yourself for exploring all the wonders of west Kerry without the crowds and expense of Killarney. Today, Killorglin is a prosperous town of around 2,200 people, with significant employment in financial services and pharmaceuticals, but it still has the feel of a nice small market town with plenty to see and do in the nearby area.

During the Norman period, Killorglin developed at the last crossing of the River Laune before it empties into Castlemaine Harbour and then Dingle Bay. The Laune, which begins its journey at the Lakes of Killarney, is an impressive sight as it rushes through the town – and it has long attracted anglers from Ireland and further afield. Killorglin's most impressive building, visible at one end of Market Street, is St James's Catholic church. Like so many other Kerry churches, it was built in the turbulent years of the 1880s, and like its cousin in Cahersiveen, its tower was never finished. Nearby, where there is now a large car park, was the site of one of the most important cattle markets in Kerry. When the railway was built from Farranfore to Cahersiveen in the 1880s, a major source of revenue came from the live export of cows to Dublin and then onwards to the English market. The large metal railway viaduct built at this time at the northern edge of the town is now a popular scenic walk.

For most Irish people, Killorglin means Puck Fair (*Aonach an Phoic*, 'fair of the male goat'). Held each year on 10–12 August, its roots can be traced back at least as far as the early 1600s, and in some ways it has not changed all that much since; one guidebook from almost two centuries ago describes it as a festival where 'a male goat is sometimes ornamented and paraded about the fair'. The sequence of events in recent years is that a male goat, sourced from the nearby mountains, is brought into Killorglin and crowned 'King Puck' by a girl from one of the local schools. The goat is then hoisted atop a platform in the centre of the town for three days amid great fanfare, music and festivities. If you are visiting Killorglin at quieter times of the year, you can see a large statue of 'King Puck' at one end of the bridge.

For history buffs, Killorglin is the birthplace of the Irish republican Tom Barry (1897–1980), the son of a police officer. His memoir, *Guerilla Days in Ireland* (1949), remains one of the classic accounts of the Irish War of Independence. He is buried in Cork city. Furthermore, at Ballykissane pier, 2km north of Killorglin, there is a monument to the three Irish Volunteers who drowned accidentally in 1916 while involved in a plot to land German weapons ahead of the Easter Rising (see also Tralee, Banna Strand, p.65).

Beyond Killorglin, there is much to see and do including:

Killarney (*Cill Airne*), a 30-minute drive. Killarney has been the headquarters of Irish tourism for as long as that term has existed. Between the town and the surroundings – lakes, woods, mountains – there is no shortage of wonderful days out to be enjoyed.

The Gap of Dunloe, a 20-minute drive. Along with Killarney, a very famous rugged mountain pass, the Gap of Dunloe is best enjoyed by pony and trap (driving is not advised). Kate Kearney's Cottage is the local haunt for pints and food.

Inch beach, a 30-minute drive. The bigger sister to Rossbeigh Strand (see Cahersiveen, p.70), Inch beach offers limitless sand and sea with views of the mountainous Iveragh and Dingle peninsulas.

Crag Cave, near Castleisland, a 30-minute drive. If the coastal roads are too busy with tourists, or the weather is poor, head inland for Crag Cave, extensive limestone caves set up for family visits. Most schoolchildren from Cork and Kerry are brought there at some point, and I still have vivid memories of the dramatic stalactites and stalagmites.

IMAGES Right: Statue in honour of Killorglin's famous 'King Puck'.
Middle left: Pony and trap tours are popular with visitors at the Gap of Dunloe.
Middle right: With its picturesque setting, Killarney has long been a popular tourist destination.
Bottom: Surfers on Inch beach.

CAHERSIVEEN

CAHERSIVEEN (*CATHAIR SAIDHBHÍN*). Like Belmullet and Clifden, Cahersiveen has the feel of a frontier town, still a little new and raw. From Dublin to here is about as long a drive as it gets in Ireland – a full four and a half hours. This remoteness is immediately obvious if you take a glance at a historic Ordnance Survey map of the town; drawn around 1840, it shows a road bridge 'in progress', a 'new quay' under construction, and a single main street with the basic prerequisites of any new Irish town – courthouse, prison, Catholic chapel, post office. The town grew from just five houses in 1815 to around 1,500 people by the 1840s, spurred on by the building of a new road to Valentia Harbour. Even the name itself has more uncertainty than usual in Ireland. You can take your pick of 'i's and 'e's, 's's and 'c's in how you spell it. In truth, the only correct spelling is in the Irish language: *Cathair Saidhbhin*, meaning 'little Sadhbh's stone ringfort'.

Cahersiveen is today a small town situated on the south side of the Fertha river, several kilometres upstream of Valentia Harbour. Its marina is quite well sheltered and offers much better protection for visiting sailors than Knightstown or Portmagee. Most of the lively pubs and best restaurants are located on the town's old main street, now the N70 'Ring of Kerry' route. The French café Petit Delice is particularly recommended. Nearby, it's hard to miss the remarkable Catholic church, built in a stern Gothic style and with a clearly unfinished tower. This was begun in the 1880s and is highly unusual in Ireland in being named after a lay person: its full dedication, appropriately for a political leader best known for the emancipation of Irish Catholics in the 1820s, is 'The Daniel O'Connell Memorial Church of the Holy Cross' (see also Sneem, p.72).

Cahersiveen's skyline is dominated by an intriguing building: a huge Royal Irish Constabulary (police) barracks built near the river in the 1870s. Now a heritage centre, its looming presence was an undeniable statement to the local Fenians and nationalists of the strength of British rule. In 1922, anti-Treaty IRA forces made their own views known by torching the building, leaving it a dramatic ruin until it was reconstructed in the 1990s. Nearby is a lengthy metal viaduct, formerly the termination of a long and dramatic railway line along the peninsula from Killorglin (closed in 1960).

Cahersiveen is surrounded by wonderfully remote landscapes of mountains, islands, cliffs and water. Each August, over a long weekend, the town hosts a large Festival of Music and the Arts. For those seeking solitude, a short distance to the north of the bridge, you will find the Leacanabuaile and Cahergall stone forts, which allow you to imagine life here 1,000–1,500 years ago. Nearby, there is a marked Pilgrim Trail up *Cnoc na dTobar* (690m), offering panoramic views of the whole area. Further beyond there are numerous options for great days out, including:

Valentia Island (derived from *Béal Inse*, pronounced va-lin-cha *not* va-lin-cia (no connection to the city in Spain!)), a 30-minute journey via the bridge at Portmagee or the car ferry to Knightstown. Here you will find a large former slate quarry with a grotto in it, tetrapod footprints dating back 385 million years, the site where the first transatlantic telegraph cable came ashore from Newfoundland in 1858, and a dramatic walk up Bray Head with its high cliffs and ruined Napoleonic-era signal tower.

Skellig Michael (*Sceilg Mhichíl*), 12km offshore, accessible by boat from Portmagee and elsewhere. The famous UNESCO World Heritage Site monastery dating back to at least the eighth century is situated on a lonely rock in the wild Atlantic. The raw grandeur of this place defies words. It's not for those who suffer from seasickness or from fear of heights.

Rossbeigh Strand, a 30-minute drive through the mountains. This vast sandy beach with big waves and big views at the head of Dingle bay is an antidote to a rough day at sea visiting the Skelligs.

IMAGES Top left: The Daniel O'Connell Memorial Church of the Holy Cross in Cahersiveen.
Top right: The imposing former RIC barracks is now a heritage centre.
Middle left: Dingle bay from the road linking Killorglin with Cahersiveen.
Lower middle left: The former slate quarry on Valentia Island now houses a grotto.
Bottom: Leacanabuaile stone fort.

SNEEM

SNEEM (*AN tSNAIDHM*). The Iveragh peninsula, perhaps best known as the 'Ring of Kerry' route, is one of the most sparsely populated parts of Ireland. In total, around 20,000 people live here. To put that into some perspective, Iveragh has around the same number of people per square kilometre (about 15) as the US state of Utah and is less densely packed than Iowa. Yet the towns and villages, few and far between, are quite tightly packed and can feel very busy, especially in the summer months. Sneem is at the smaller end of Kerry villages, home to a permanent population of around 500 people. Its name comes from the Irish *An tSnaidhm*, which means simply 'the knot' – well suited to a coastal village with such a sheltered anchorage. There are, however, varying interpretations locally as to the origins of this name, and my personal favourite is that it comes from the swirling currents in the water where the mountain river falls over jagged rocks and meets the sea just below the town.

Sneem is the perfect base for exploring the southern half of Iveragh. The town's layout is unusual in that it has two small triangular greens at opposite ends, each with terraces of well-preserved and colourful two-storey houses. Each November, over a long weekend, its pubs and hotels host a big Storytelling and Folklore Festival. For those interested in architecture, the unusual Church of Ireland church to the west of the river dates mostly from the early nineteenth century and has a striking octagonal tower. Nearby is St Michael's, the town's Catholic church, built in the 1860s in a full-blooded Italian style of architecture. It was paid for by the noted archaeologist Edwin Wyndham-Quin, the third earl of Dunraven, who fell in love with the islands near Sneem. On the adjacent Quay Road is the Sneem Sculpture Park.

The Sneem river opens out to Kenmare bay about 3km south of the town. Nearby is the top-of-the-market Parknasilla Hotel, formerly a Great Southern Hotel owned by the Irish state railway company. In the summer months, Parknasilla and the nearby islands attract visitors from near and far.

It would be possible to spend a month in Sneem and not run out of extraordinary and breathtaking daytrips. Give yourself plenty of time to get around as the roads are narrow and windy. Some highlights include:

Staigue Stone Fort, a 25-minute drive. An exceptionally large Irish ring fort with 4-metre-thick stone ramparts, dating from the early centuries AD and offering majestic views of the mountains and the sea. There is a modest admission charge.

Derrynane, a 30-minute drive. Derrynane House was the home of Daniel O'Connell, the great nineteenth-century Irish political leader. Now owned by the state, it is open to the public. Nearby is the wonderful Derrynane beach and harbour, from where boat trips can be organised to see some of the many remote islands, including the Skelligs.

IMAGES Below, top: A colourful terrace of houses lining one of Sneem's triangular greens.
Bottom: Derrynane House was the home of Daniel O'Connell.
Opposite, top: Sneem is ideally situated for exploring the southern half of the Ring of Kerry.
Opposite, bottom: The ramparts of the ancient Staigue Fort are 4 metres thick in places.

SNEEM

Waterville, a 45-minute drive. The only other town of any size between Kenmare and Cahersiveen, Waterville hosts the Charlie Chaplin Comedy Film Festival each August and numerous cycling, running and swimming events throughout the summer.

Kerry International Dark-Sky Reserve, centred on Lough Currane near Waterville, a 45-minute drive. Established in 2014, the reserve promises crystal-clear views of the night sky (when it's not raining!).

Ballaghisheen Pass, a 50-minute drive. There are only three roads that run east–west across the Iveragh peninsula, and two of them form the busy, touristy coastal 'Ring of Kerry' route. The third runs down the peninsula's spine from Glencar near Carrauntoohil to Waterville via the Ballaghisheen Pass. It is spectacularly remote and is recommended as a good but challenging cycle.

Carrauntoohil (*Corrán Tuathail*), Ireland's highest mountain, a 1-hour drive (to the car park at Lisleibane). Part of the extensive MacGillycuddy's Reeks, Carrauntoohil rises to 1,038 metres. See local maps and guides before planning your hike.

KENMARE

KENMARE (*CEANN MARA/AN NEIDÍN*). Kerry's most famous town is Killarney, but I would prefer Kenmare any day. It is filled with history, culture and good food, and the sea is only a few minutes away. Within a reasonably short drive can be found some of Ireland's most enchanting mountain valleys and harbours. Today home to around 2,500 people, Kenmare derives its English name from *Ceann mara*, literally the head of the sea – the head of Kenmare bay – but its old Irish name is much more evocative: *An Neidín*, the little nest. And though most of the town dates from only the nineteenth century (new by Irish standards), its neat triangular layout and attractive tree-lined green gives it the feel of a cosy, well-planned outpost among the great wildness of the southwest of Ireland.

Kenmare is a classic market town, for a long time owned and managed by a single big landlord who lived in England, the Marquess of Lansdowne; at its peak, the family owned over 90,000 acres in the surrounding area. The locals are rightly proud of their beautiful town and will be quick to tell you that it regularly wins awards at the annual Irish Tidy Towns competition. Though the traffic is often heavy in the summer months, the main streets, normally festooned with Kerry flags, are pleasant to walk and offer a remarkable variety of pubs, cafés, restaurants, and antique shops. My personal favourite for a special treat is The Lime Tree restaurant (regularly booked out in the summer months), where you can taste the finest local seafood by candlelight in an old stone schoolhouse built in the 1830s, then adjourn to a nearby pub for traditional music and singing.

IMAGES Opposite, top: Storm clouds threaten on the remote Ballaghisheen Pass.
Opposite, bottom: The MacGillycuddy Reeks as seen from Carrauntoohil, Ireland's highest mountain.
Right: A colourful street corner in Kenmare.

Kenmare is, in short, well accustomed to tourism: long before the 'Wild Atlantic Way', it was on the map as the southeastern corner of the popular 180km 'Ring of Kerry' driving and cycling route. If arriving from Glengarriff, you will pass over Kenmare sound on a grand 1930s arched bridge. As you drive over it, spare a thought for those who came this way in the early twentieth century across its predecessor: a wobbly, rickety, unstable iron suspension bridge put up in the 1830s (probably Ireland's first large suspension bridge), so dangerous that it was eventually closed to traffic and replaced by the current structure! On the Kenmare side of the bridge is the sculptor Dick Joynt's 'The Music Makers', three large limestone statues looking out over the sea.

Although it is tempting to head straight for the mountains and the sea, it's worth spending time in the town itself. On Wednesdays, from 10am to 4pm, the local farmer's market takes over the square by the Fair Green. In the autumn, the town hosts the Small Roads Theatre Festival in its former Carnegie Library, and also the 'Halloween Howl'. The town's two main churches – St Patrick's (Church of Ireland) and Holy Cross (Catholic) – were built in the 1850s–1860s, and until recently the Poor Clare nuns had a convent in the town, known for its hand-made lace.

The countryside around Kenmare forms one of the most popular tourist hotspots in Ireland, and for good reason. There is a wealth of things to do and see, including:

Seafari tours, from the pier to the south of the town. This is your gateway to Kenmare bay, its islands, seals, dolphins and eagles.

Gleninchaquin Park, a 25-minute drive. Here you will find extensive walking trails through a working farm, with spectacular views of waterfalls at the surrounding Caha mountains. Accommodation is available.

Derreen Gardens, Lauragh, a 25-minute drive. The lush gardens at Derreen are one of the great treasures of the southwest of Ireland. Nearby is Kilmacillogue Harbour (Bunaw), where accommodation, fresh seafood and pints are available at Helen's Bar, best enjoyed sitting out on the pier on a summer's evening.

Rabach's Glen walk (Cummeengeera valley), including Shronebirrane stone circle, a 35-minute drive. This desolate valley has a dark history of robbery, murder and intrigue. You will also find the ruins of old cottages where a recluse lived until the 1950s–1960s. Parking is available for a small charge.

Mangerton Mountain, a 40-minute drive. Mangerton (An Mhangarta, 'the long-haired mountain' rises to 838 metres and offers big views of the Kerry mountains and the lakes of Killarney. Parking is available near Torc Waterfall and elsewhere.

IMAGES Opposite page: Kenmare's arched bridge dates from the 1930s.
Top left: Dick Joynt's sculpture, 'The Music Makers', stands close to the bridge in Kenmare.
Top right: Kilmacillogue Harbour, where accommodation and fresh seafood are available.
Middle: The lush gardens of Derreen at Lauragh.
Bottom: Ruins of old cottages in the remote Rabach's Glen with the peak of Bireca above.

ALLIHIES

ALLIHIES (*NA hAILICHÍ*). Almost all my impressions of Allihies are of the village at night. This is when it truly comes alive and turns into the perfect stopping-off place after a long day of hiking or cycling in the surrounding hills. Its two music-filled pubs fill up rapidly with the rich variety of locals and blow-ins from all around the world who have made the spectacular outer reaches of the Beara Peninsula their home. On Sunday evenings, a group of local musicians and singers annex half of O'Neill's – and they extend a warm welcome to any musically inclined visitor who wishes to join. If that's not you, sit back, relax, and enjoy the jigs, fresh seafood and excellent pints of Murphy's stout.

The village of Allihies has a curious relationship with its environs. It grew organically and somewhat chaotically in the early nineteenth century to serve the nearby copper mines. But the village's centre is well back from the sea and so its character is different from other nearby fishing towns – its little beach is windswept at the best of times. The great amphitheatre of water hemmed in by the jagged rocky ridges on both sides – Ballydonegan Bay – offers no shelter to a visiting sailboat, which must instead seek a safe anchorage in Castletownbere or further afield. This is the Wild Atlantic at its wildest and most inhospitable – and one consequence is that Allihies faces into the hills more than out to the sea. To best appreciate the beauty of this part of Beara, pull in by the viewing point near the top of the road that heads south from Allihies to Dursey and Castletownbere, especially around sunrise or sunset.

You will see near the village the ruins and mineshafts left by the search for copper, which came and went in fits and starts between 1812 and the 1880s. Its good years helped the local magnates, the Puxleys, to build Dunboy Castle; its bad years spurred many hundreds of unemployed men to emigrate to Butte, Montana – one of the largest copper-mining towns in the American West. Today, Butte has more Irish-Americans for its size (a quarter of the population) than any other city in the United States, and there continue to be strong connections with Allihies – including several locals from Beara who have made the journey to the Rocky Mountains to reconnect with their distant relatives.

Allihies is the most westerly village of any size on the Beara Peninsula, and arriving there by car or especially by bicycle gives a satisfying sense of having made it to the end of a long journey. The village is busiest on and around 15 August – when the main festival is staged. Don't be surprised if, on your visit, the locals want to know who you are, where you have come from, and where you are going!

Any visitor would need little convincing to stay in Allihies a long time. Among the highlights are:

Allihies Copper Mine Museum, in the village. Opened in 2007. A short walk or drive north of the village gives close-up views of one of the old engine houses.

IMAGES Opposite: Horse racing at the Allihies festival.
Top: Dursey Island, the Cow Rock and the Bull Rock as seen from Cod's Head near Allihies.
Bottom left: An old engine rooms of a mineshaft stands as a reminder of the industry from which the village grew.
Middle right: Bare rock and the remains of the former mines form the backdrop to the village of Allihies.
Bottom right: The lighthouse on the Bull Rock as seen from Allihies.

SERENE
WT 342
MICHELE J.

Dursey Island, including Dursey Sound and Cable-car, a 20-minute drive. Dursey makes for one of the most spectacular and memorable hikes in Ireland. It is connected to the mainland by a cable-car (very busy in the summer months) over the treacherous waters of Dursey Sound. If you see boats sailing unusually close to the island, they are in fact wisely avoiding a dangerous submerged rock mid-channel. Beyond Dursey are the Calf, Cow, and Bull Rocks and the Skelligs in the distance.

Walks, in all directions from the village. One particularly scenic walk is from the village all the way to Dursey Sound, which takes in dramatic cliff views and the beautiful sandy beach at Garnish.

Eyeries (*Na hAoraí*), a 25-minute drive. This small picture-perfect village is famous for its colourful houses, with spectacular routes leading out to Kilcatherine Point and beyond.

CASTLETOWNBERE

CASTLETOWN BEREHAVEN (*BAILE CHAISLEÁIN BHÉARRA*). Castletownbere is a sensible, practical, no-nonsense kind of town that offers welcome respite from the more touristy stop-offs in Cork and Kerry. Like other fishing ports such as Killybegs, Castletownbere has had its ups and downs over the years. The great volume of fish landed here is generally now exported to other parts of the European Union – look out for those refrigerated lorries that ply the narrow peninsula road at night! The town itself was designed for the fishing industry: beyond its single main street and small square (where most of the pubs and restaurants are located) are its expansive quays, yards, warehouses and fisheries school. The scale of industrial fishing in Castletownbere is sometimes hard to appreciate but you can get a sense of it by taking a short walk along the quays where space is so tight that you may see thirty or more huge trawlers stern-tied next to each other, pointing out into the Atlantic like an armada ready to set sail.

The only constant in Castletownbere's long history has been its excellent natural anchorage, fully sheltered from the ocean by the hills of Bere Island. Everything else, like the tide, has ebbed and flowed. The old official name for the town – Castletown Berehaven – speaks to its strategic importance as a

IMAGES Opposite, top: Dursey Island is connected to the mainland by the only cable-car service in Ireland.
Opposite, bottom left: A quiet pier at Kilcatherine near the village of Eyeries.
Opposite, bottom right: Colourful fishing boats sheltering near Eyeries.
Below: The busy fishing port of Castletownbere.

safe harbour on the south-western coast. 'Bere' here comes from O'Sullivan Beare, the Gaelic aristocratic family married into Spanish nobility who built Dunboy Castle near the town. This castle was subjected to a deadly siege by English forces in 1602, a catastrophe that marked the passing of a political and cultural epoch. Its evocative ruins are a reminder of the complex history of Spanish and English involvement in west Cork. Much later, Berehaven became a favourite safe harbour for the British navy, and after the French attempted to land in 1796, Bere Island was fortified with Martello towers, some of which survive and may be visited.

Bere Island is a tranquil paradise and the perfect place for a long hike. It is big by Irish standards, measuring about 10km long and 2km wide, and there are separate ferry services running from its western and eastern ends. Barracks and firing ranges near the latter speak to its curious history as one of the three 'treaty ports' kept by Britain after the creation of the Free State in the 1920s. In September 1938, the British forces finally left, sparing the island from almost certain bombing during the war that soon followed. The removal of British forces was popular in the country at large at the time but, locally, it meant the end of a lucrative provisions trade. Seán Ó Faoláin, in his bleak *Irish Journey* (1940), wrote of Beara having 'sunk back into its own natural primitiveness' when the navy weighed anchor and left.

In the summer you may find it sunny in Bantry or Kenmare but misty in Castletown. But there's still plenty to enjoy in the town and nearby, including:

The Sarah Walker Gallery, in the town. This contemporary art gallery opened in the early years of the twenty-first century in a former carriage-house by the sea. It is open every day in the summer and at weekends in the winter.

IMAGES Opposite: A restored Martello tower on Bere Island.
Top: An early nineteenth-century signal tower at Black Ball Head on the Beara Peninsula.
Above: Ardnakinna Lighthouse on the western entrance to Castletownbere.

Dunboy (*Dún Baoi*), a 10-minute drive. In the summer months, sail boats anchor in this beautiful little bay. In addition to the ruined O'Sullivan Beare castle, you will find nearby the former Puxley mansion built with the profits of copper mining. The house was burnt by the IRA in 1920, partially rebuilt and then messily abandoned once more in recent years. It is an extraordinary Victorian fantasy now in need of love and attention.

Dzogchen Beara, a 15-minute drive. This Tibetan Buddhist meditation and retreat centre was founded in 1987. If you have visited Beara but missed out on the views here over the Atlantic you will just need to come back! Accommodation is available.

Healy Pass, a 25-minute drive. This dramatic mountain pass was named after the prominent nationalist Tim Healy, first Governor-General of the Irish Free State. The pass is a well-known cycling challenge and gives spectacular views of the Caha mountains and Glanmore lake (on the Kerry side). Ice-creams are sometimes available at the summit.

IMAGES Above: Hungry Hill from the southern approaches to the Healy Pass.
Opposite: Old trees and lush vegetation at Dunboy near Castletownbere.

GLENGARRIFF

GLENGARRIFF (*AN GLEANN GARBH*). The village of Glengarriff is almost incidental to the landscape that surrounds it, the most ubiquitous feature of which is rock. Great expanses of jagged old red sandstone dominate the area, emerging like huge erratic blocks in the village itself: near a pub, behind the doctor's surgery, even scattered among the headstones in the cemetery. This dramatic landscape has brought tourists from all around the world for longer than most parts of Ireland except perhaps Killarney, and even today the village has a distinctly touristy feel to it. In the early nineteenth century, the White family of Bantry House developed the area as a picture-perfect getaway. They planted hundreds of acres of oak woodland and built a hunting lodge and a great faux-Gothic castle in the romantic spirit of that time; the castle survives, appropriately enough in a semi-ruinous state, and can be spotted from on board the ferry to Garnish Island. A substantial hotel in the village soon followed; it was later expanded and still operates as the Eccles Hotel, in honour of its first owner, Thomas Eccles. Glengarriff became a mandatory stop-off on what became known as the 'Prince of Wales Route' through Cork and Kerry, a journey made all the easier by the building of new roads over the hills and later railway and steamship services via Bantry.

For me, Glengarriff is a perfect place to enjoy a drink after a day out hiking or sailing. The centre of the village is the road junction framed by the brightly painted O'Shea's Post Office and Shop on one side and the Blue Loo Pub on the other. The benches outside the Blue Loo are soaked in evening sunshine and seated there you can watch the passing traffic divide between the coast road and the mountain pass to Kerry known for its bare-rock tunnels. These were cut almost two centuries ago and remain almost untouched today. If planning a cycle, remember to check your lights beforehand and keep an eye out for torrents of water (especially in the winter). As you leave Glengarriff to begin the climb up over the Caha hills, you will see the village's pretty little Gothic Catholic church (built 1902) to your right.

Most of the village life happens on its single busy main street, but only a short walk down towards the sea reveals a tranquil haven of old Scots Pine and rhododendron on a bend in a river, downstream of a half-ruined ancient bridge – an area known as the Poulgorm (or blue pool) Nature Park and Coastal Woodland Walk. Here you will find a series of trails through the lush natural landscape and secluded bays and inlets. Ferries depart from Poulgorm for Garnish Island.

Glengarriff is such a well-developed tourist location that any list of nearby things to see and do has to be highly selective, but no visit would be complete without seeing at least a couple of the following:

Garnish Island (*Ilnacullin*), a 15-minute boat journey from various departure points in the village and nearby. Originally little more than a Martello Tower (1805) built on a rocky island, Garnish Island (Ilancullin) was transformed into an Italian garden of international importance in the years just before the First World War. Its elegant classical buildings and exotic plants still provide quite a surprise to any visitor. The island was given to the state in the early 1950s.

The Beara Way, from the village. This is an extensive hiking trail in the Caha range. If you would prefer a mental rather than a physical challenge, try to pronounce the names of two of the larger lakes in these mountains: Derreenadarodia (de-reen-a-da-voda, often shortened to 'twelve-cow lake') and Eekenohoolikeaghaun (a-heena-hoona-gay-gone, somewhat more of a mystery).

Glengarriff Nature Reserve (Glengarriff Woods), a 5-minute drive. Almost as famous as Garnish Island (Ilnacullin), these woods were planted by the White family two centuries ago and are now in public ownership. The canopy is mostly Sessile Oaks and extends for hundreds of acres. There are many marked walkways, including a steep ascent to a rocky outcrop known as 'Lady Bantry's Lookout'. Be careful where you park – the river rises rapidly after heavy rains (as the warning signs will tell you).

IMAGES Top: Poulgorm Nature Park and Coastal Woodland Walk, Glengarriff.
Middle left: The colourful main street in Glengarriff.
Bottom left: The elegant Italian garden on Garnish Island (Ilnacullin).
Bottom right: Glengarriff's pretty Catholic church dates from 1902.

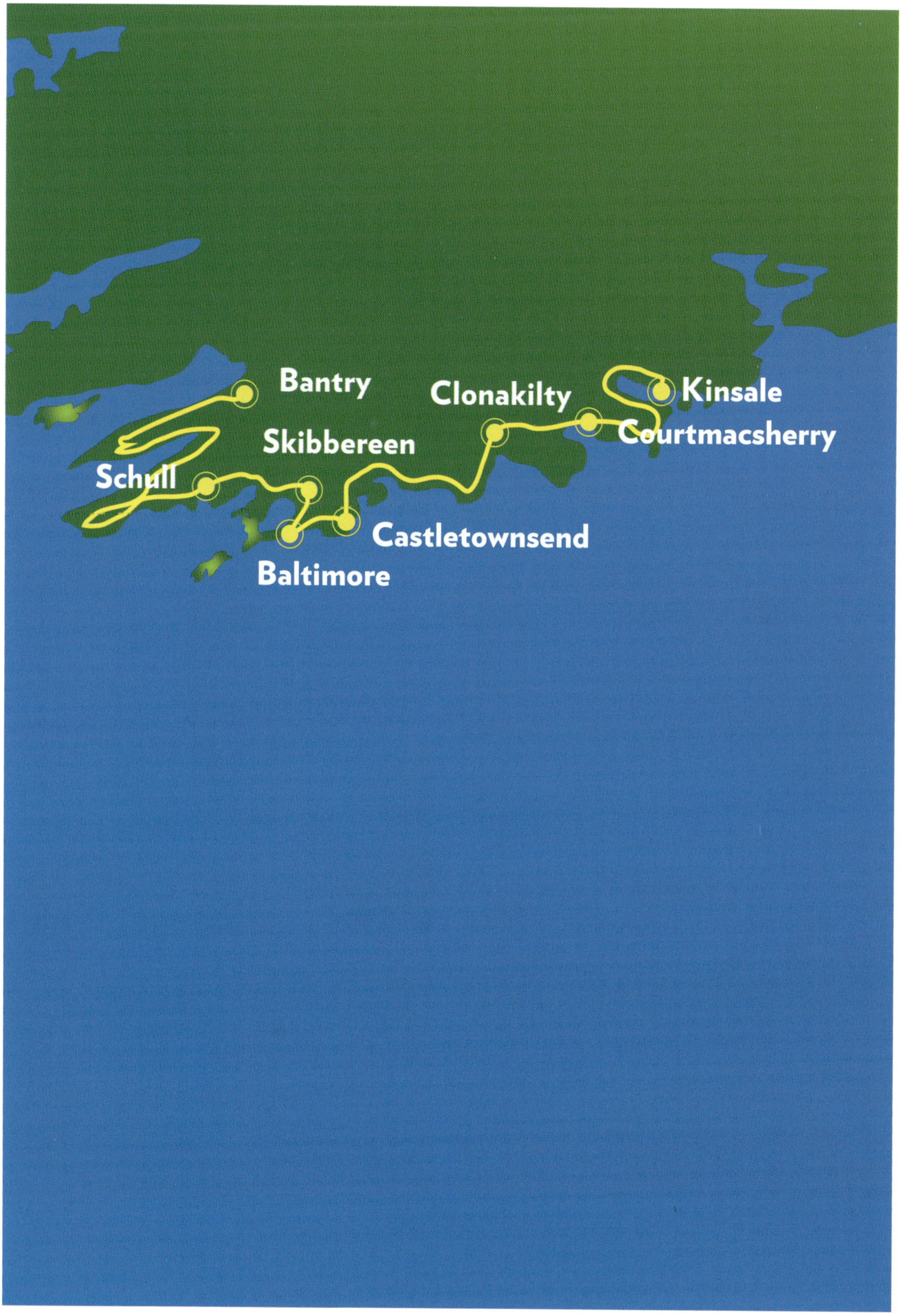
Bantry
Clonakilty
Kinsale
Skibbereen
Courtmacsherry
Schull
Castletownsend
Baltimore

BANTRY TO KINSALE

Dramatic cliffs at Mizen Head.

BANTRY

BANTRY (*BEANNTRAÍ*). Bantry is all about the sea. Hills surround and envelop the town's streets in the same way as the rocky mountains frame the bay onto which it opens. Every coastal Irish town has its own character, and for Bantry it's this relationship between the energy of its narrow streets and the open expanse of water. Nowhere is this more obvious than on the large elevated square, frequently blasted with south-westerly winds. On Fridays – especially on the first Friday of the month and throughout the summer – the Square is transformed into one of Ireland's best open markets, offering everything from the organic food and ingredients from the surrounding valleys to construction machinery, books, and even hens and ducks. If you leave your car parked there the night before, you may come back to find it surrounded – and integrated – into the day's proceedings. On 'Fair Day', look out for the visiting antique dealers who unload their trucks filled with house clear-outs, quickly divvied up among the local expert collectors. If the crowds become too much, or the wind is up, the shelter of Bantry's maze of hilly one-way streets will offer easy respite. There are countless good restaurants and cafés

dotted throughout the Bantry, and at least a dozen proper, authentic Cork pubs. If you are interested in architecture, check out St Brendan's or St. Finbarr's churches, the dramatic brutalist 1970s library erected by a waterfall, or the historic ruined church and graveyard at Garryvurcha.

Bantry is, almost literally, awash with history. In the 1790s, the French attempted to invade, only to be scattered in storms (they arrived in December). Soon after, the British military built vast fortifications to protect the bay, the remains of which are easily spotted. Overlooking the inner harbour – now, as then – is Bantry House and Gardens, which no visitor to the area should miss. The view from atop the one-hundred steps behind the house is perhaps the grandest in all of Ireland. The Shelswell-Whites, who still live in the house, welcome visitors and host major international events including the West Cork Chamber Music Festival each summer.

Bantry's uniqueness is reflected in its relationship with Whiddy Island, only a ten-minute boat trip from the main pier. In recent years, Whiddy has been transformed with walking routes, bicycles for hire, summer music and plays, and – most of all – its very own pub, where Tim and Eileen serve food and pints to locals and visitors alike. The old schoolhouse has recently been turned into a hostel. Whiddy is an essential stop-off on any visit to west Cork and its rich history is worthy of a book of its own. Make sure to visit those dramatic fortifications built to send a stern warning to the French. At the western end of the island is a large oil-storage terminal, where much of Ireland's national reserves are kept. Out to sea, you will spot an abandoned, half-ruined jetty, the sombre monument to the explosion of the Betelgeuse oil tanker in 1979, which claimed fifty-one lives. Locals recount the terrifying blasts that shook windows in the Westlodge Hotel that night, and the sizeable chunks of steel from the ship that were thrown into the air and landed in the backyards of houses throughout the town.

IMAGES Opposite, top: The view from behind Bantry House is one of the grandest in the country.
Opposite, middle: An anchor in the town square was salvaged from one of the French ships involved in the attempted invasion in 1796.
Opposite, bottom: Sunset over Bantry Bay and the Caha hills on the Beara Peninsula.
Above: Bantry is surrounded by hills on three sides.

Bantry rewards a lengthy stay. Once you have seen the big house and walked the length of Whiddy Island, the surrounding countryside offers memorable daytrips, including:

Mealagh Valley, a 10-minute drive. This is perfect for a day's cycling on quiet roads. Some steep climbs are available!

Drimoleague Walkways, a 20-minute drive. You can take your pick of a comprehensive network of walkways by the River Ilen, built and maintained by an enthusiastic local community.

Sheep's Head Peninsula, a 20-minute drive. Dozens of marked walks criss-cross this narrow but hilly peninsula, including a 27km route along the entire ridge. It is also possible to park near the end and walk to a small lighthouse nestled among cliffs.

Gougane Barra, a 35-minute drive. A sheltered hiking route in bad weather in a valley of unparalleled natural beauty, the source of the River Lee. Gougane has been a site of religious pilgrimage for over a thousand years.

SCHULL

SCHULL (*SCOIL MHUIRE*). My childhood memories of Schull are of a quiet village with not very much happening. Now this has all changed: perhaps more than any other village in the area, Schull has boomed with the influx of visitors in the summer months. It is still sleepy in the darkest of winter but between June and September, you will find it almost overrun with crowds, campervans, caravans and cyclists.

Schull is all about the water, and the hustle and bustle of the town recedes quickly as you head out into the harbour on a boat or kayak. The town serves as the main gateway for a multitude of water sports in Roaringwater Bay, most notably sailing races between and among its many islands. Upwards of 100 ocean-going boats take part in some of these events – for example, racing out to the Fastnet lighthouse and back. The bay can be treacherous for those not familiar with its many small islands and submerged rocks, and you may overhear rumours in the shoreside cafés of damaged keels or worse still. There's an old saying in Roaringwater bay that there are sailors who have hit rocks, and there are liars.

IMAGES Below: Abandoned houses on the Sheep's Head Peninsula with Bantry Bay in the distance.
Opposite, top: Beautiful Gougane Barra has been the site of religious pilgrimage for over a thousand years.
Opposite, Middle: The dramatic remains of Castle Donovan as seen from one of the marked walks near Drimoleague.
Opposite, bottom left: Sailing boats often race from Schull out to the Fastnet Lighthouse and back.
Opposite, bottom right: Schull's harbour is busy with recreational boating in the summer months.

IMAGES Top: Ballydehob's twelve-arch stone railway viaduct dates from the nineteenth century.
Bottom left: Barley Cove near Mizen Head.
Bottom right: Medieval castles at Three Castle Head on the Mizen Peninsula.

Those who called Schull their home in distant times past could never have predicted how successful the town would become as a tourist centre, for Schull was long synonymous with poverty. For many centuries, the only business was in small-scale fishing. The unusual name is derived from *Scoil Mhuire*, 'Mary's school'. Older maps sometimes chose the harsh-sounding 'Skull', but that does little justice to its proper placename in the Irish language. The town's darkest days were undoubtedly during the Great Famine of 1845–1852, when the macabre undertones of 'Skull' featured in British press coverage of the terrible loss of life here. Such was the scale of destitution that during these years an extra workhouse was built on the outskirts of the village. Today, ruined buildings, ivy-clad walls and a plaque mark its former location on the road to Ballydehob, serving as a sombre memorial to the 40 per cent of the population of the area who died or emigrated during these years.

A mecca for art, culture, music, food, and the outdoors, the Schull of today is a very different place. You have a choice, too, between hills and islands, with lots of hiking and cycling routes on and near Mount Gabriel to the north, where copper was once mined (its white domes form part of a radar system for air traffic control). Alternatively, to the south, it is only a short kayak trip to the islands. Further out to sea, you will spot the Fastnet lighthouse (48m), perched on a lonely rock 6.5km southwest of Cape Clear. This was built with Cornish granite between 1896 and 1904, replacing an earlier tower. The last lighthouse keeper left the rock in 1989.

For daytrips beyond:

Long Island, by boat from the harbour. A population of more than 300 before the Famine has now been reduced to just a dozen. There are many other islands nearby, some of which are private retreats (ask locally before planning a trip).

Cape Clear and **Fastnet Lighthouse**. Boat trips leave from Schull on a regular basis during the summer months. Look out for dolphins and whales.

Ballydehob (*Béal an Dá Chab*, 'mouth of the two river fords'), a 10-minute drive. Straddling the estuary is a remarkable twelve-arch stone railway viaduct, built in the 1880s.

Ferries to **Heir Island**, a 25-minute drive. The short crossing departs from Cunnamore Pier. As well as a lovely island to walk, Island Cottage restaurant offers an unforgettable culinary experience (the menu is fixed).

Barley Cove and **Mizen Head**, a 25-minute drive. The best beach in the area, Barley Cove is very busy in the summer. Mizen Head is known as the most southerly point in Ireland, and is accessible by a dramatic arched bridge over a deep chasm.

Three Castle Head, a 30-minute drive. Parking is available for a modest fee. A chain of medieval castles and walls stretches from a large lake to huge cliffs, with views of the Sheep's Head and Beara peninsulas.

BALTIMORE

BALTIMORE (*DÚN NA SÉAD*). You never know who you will meet in Baltimore. As well as a popular summer tourist destination, the excellent harbour is a favourite stop-off for sailors on European and transatlantic journeys. Though the tradition of building fine wooden boats here has fallen somewhat into abeyance since the 1960s, the town is still dominated by its relationship with Roaringwater Bay and the wild Atlantic beyond.

Baltimore has been in the business of fishing and maritime trade for at least 400 years, receiving its charter from King James I in 1613. Baltimore is, an anglicisation of the Irish for, simply, 'town of the big house', a meaning better captured in its official Irish name of *Dún na Séad* or 'fort of the jewels'. Close to the pier is the old castle (mostly dating from Crooke's time), which was beautifully restored in the late 1990s and is now open to the public – it's well worth a visit.

The town is perhaps best known for a disastrous pirate raid of 1631 – the 'Sack of Baltimore', memorialised in a ballad by Thomas Davis, the nationalist and Young Irelander who also wrote the words for the famous rebel song, 'A Nation Once Again'. On the eve of the raid, there were around sixty houses in the village, the occupants of which were busy with pilchard fishing and perhaps the odd bottle of brandy. Then, on 20 June 1631, the village was sacked by Algerian pirates; many of the inhabitants were kidnapped and enslaved, most never to return to Ireland. Story, counter-story and rumour still circulate about the exact events – perhaps best debated over a drink in the Algiers Inn pub near the castle. The village only recovered in the nineteenth century, and most of the buildings date from that time onwards. An exception, though, is the beautifully ruined church at Tullagh to the east, down a lane behind Casey's Hotel. This was built as early as 1739 on a majestic site overlooking the water, from which you can also see the remains of the old railway line. The old red-brick station building survives near the pier, though it hasn't seen a train since the 1960s.

Once you have sampled the best food and drink in the centre of the town (including the Michelin-star restaurant Dede at the Customs House – if you can get a booking!) there is plenty to see and do beyond, including:

The Beacon, a 5-minute drive. Built during the Great Famine, this 15m-high, 4m-wide white landmark has guided ships to safety for many generations since. In stormy weather, the views across the channel to Sherkin Island and beyond are surely some of the most majestic and awe-inspiring in all of Ireland.

Sherkin Island, a short ferry journey from the pier. You will be dropped off by the ruins of a Franciscan friary, built in the 1460s. Though raided, burnt, and later suppressed, its church and cloister survive in remarkably good condition. Ferries from Baltimore also serve Cape Clear Island and the Fastnet (see Schull, p.95).

Whale, dolphin, and seabird boat tours, departing from the pier. Roaringwater Bay teems with wildlife both above and below water. Regular tours are arranged by environmentally friendly local companies, Whale Watch West Cork and Baltimore Sea Safari.

Diving and snorkelling, departing from the pier. There are many shipwrecks in the harbour and out to sea, including a U-boat submarine.

IMAGES Above: Ruined church and graveyard at Tullagh near Baltimore.
Below: The Baltimore Beacon with Sherkin Island in the background.
Opposite, left: Skibbereen's colourful Town Hall.
Opposite, right: The Maid of Erin monument commemorates those who died in the Irish fight for freedom.

Lough Hyne, a 15-minute drive. Declared Ireland's first marine nature reserve in the 1980s, this sea lough is beautifully situated among steep hills and old woods. The tides create rapids that can be dangerous for swimmers and kayakers but are mesmerising to sit and watch. It is best experienced off-season when not overrun with campervans!

SKIBBEREEN

SKIBBEREEN (*AN SCIOBAIRÍN*). Bantry, wrote Seán Ó Faoláin in his *Irish Journey* of 1940, 'is Skibbereen, with the fizz gone.' But what did he mean? I left Bantry and arrived in Skibbereen in search of the fizz, and I found it, to be sure, but not where I had expected. Skibbereen straddles two different images of itself. The first is the administrative town, with its government offices, its hospital, and its historic status as a cathedral town (for the diocese of Ross). Skibbereen, for example, is where you go to do your driving test, and as such the vagaries of its junctions and roundabouts are known with unusual precision for many miles around. This is the sensible, practical, fizz-less Skibbereen. The other image is a newer one – certainly not in existence when Ó Faoláin passed through eighty years ago. This is the Skibbereen that serves as a centre of gravity for the culture, food, art and music of west Cork. It really took off in the 1970s and 1980s with the arrival of so many young people from Britain, the Netherlands, and Germany, keen to escape much of the modern world. The Skibbereen Farmers' Market on Saturday mornings will give you some sense of this side of the town – though arrive early as it quickly heats up and is packed full by 11am. The 'fizz' for me was finding traders with remarkably complete collections of old American jazz on vinyl, and stacks of Nigerian fiction from the 1960s. Where else would you get it?

Few histories of Ireland omit Skibbereen. The name itself somewhat undersells the place: *An Sciobairín*, 'the little boat harbour'. The Catholic church is, in fact, a cathedral, designed in a similar style and around the same time (1820s) as many other new churches in west Cork. It was raised to pro-cathedral status in 1851 and became a full cathedral a century later. Go inside to see the elegant and crisp John Hogan monument to Bishop Michael Collins of Cloyne and Ross, who died in 1832. A generation later, Skibbereen was terribly affected by death, disease, and emigration during the Great Famine. In the Abbeystrowry graveyard to the west of the town, some 10,000 people are buried in famine pits, and many countless more in the grounds of the old workhouse to the north of the town. A visit to the Skibbereen Heritage Centre is a must for anyone who wants to learn more about the causes and consequences of this time in Irish history. Jeremiah O'Donovan Rossa, who witnessed these awful years in Skibbereen as a teenager, went on to be a central figure in Irish revolutionary nationalism through the Fenian movement.

The town bounced back quite quickly after the Famine. A large convent (now a sad ruin) was built in the 1850s–1860s, and soon afterwards the railway arrived from Cork. In the West Cork Hotel by the river, you can enjoy a drink, sitting out on the old metal viaduct that once carried trains onwards to Baltimore. With economic revival came a self-confidence that still marks Skibbereen today. As many locals will tell you, the town's newspaper, the *Skibbereen Eagle* (now incorporated in the *Southern Star*), made itself known wide and far for its claim that it would be keeping its eye on the Tsar of Russia. There must have been many shaky knees in Saint Petersburg!

The main festival – the Skibbereen Arts Festival – happens at the end of July and attracts a large and international crowd. Beyond the town there is plenty to do and see, including:

West Cork Distillers, near the mart. The comings and goings at the mart are well worth watching in their own right, but this new distillery, set up by locals, is a rising star in the area. Visits are possible by arrangement.

Tragumna beach, a 10-minute drive. This is a popular spot for swimming, though wild and dangerous in strong winds. The Skibbereen Eagle pub, named after the newspaper, offers ample respite.

All Saints Church, Drimoleague, a 15-minute drive. A showcase in modernist architecture, this church was built in the early 1950s. Inside you will find a dramatic series of stained-glass windows by Harry Clarke Studios, depicting everyday life in rural Ireland at the time.

CASTLETOWNSEND

CASTLETOWNSEND (*BAILE AN CHAISLEÁIN*). There are few towns along the south Cork coast that have a grid-like arrangement of straight streets – narrow lanes are so much more common. Castletownsend is an exception to this rule. It was clearly laid out in one go – deliberately, carefully, and to take best advantage of a long sloping hill down to the water. Where its two main streets meet stands an elegant Georgian townhouse and the 'two trees' – a pair of sycamores growing in the middle of the road, leaving just enough space to get a car past. Everything about Castletownsend is lovely and rewarding, from the preservation of so many historic buildings to the unparalleled beauty of its natural harbour, Castlehaven.

Frank Keohane, in his *Buildings of Ireland* guide for Cork, describes Castletownsend as 'a highly evocative place, redolent of Anglo-Irish society during its swansong'. Most visitors associate the town with the writer and artist Edith Somerville (1858–1949), who along with her cousin, Violet Martin (1862–1915), a.k.a. 'Martin Ross', formed the celebrated literary duo of 'Somerville and Ross'. Their *Some Experiences of an Irish R.M.* [resident magistrate], published in 1899, captures a particular moment in Anglo-Irish life as they saw it. You won't find any better place to read their work than in the wonderful gardens of Drishane House where Somerville once lived. Tom and Jane Somerville welcome visitors to their house, garden, and museum at different times of the year – check in advance for their exact opening times.

IMAGES Top: Tragumna Bay. The West Cork coastline offers dozens of popular swimming spots.
Middle: Stained-glass windows at All Saints Church, Drimoleague, designed in the 1950s.
Bottom, left: The graceful old stone bridge next to Abbeystrowry graveyard, where some 10,000 people are buried in famine pits.
Bottom, right: Historic architecture and natural beauty come together at Castletownsend.

I BAPTISE THEE
IN
THE NAME OF THE FATHER
AND
OF THE SON
AND OF THE HOLY GHOST
HOLY MARY
PRAY FOR
US SINNERS
I AM
THE BREAD OF LIFE
SUFFER LITTLE CHILDREN
TO COME UNTO ME
MAKE THE WAY KNOWN TO ME
WHEREIN I SHOULD WALK
MY LORD
AND MY GOD
DO ALL
TO THE GLORY OF GOD

Castletownsend (*Baile an Chaisleáin*, 'town of the castle' in Irish), is named after Richard Townsend, who built a castle by the water in the seventeenth century – this too can be visited. Many years later, a descendant, the Rev. Horatio Townsend (1750–1837) wrote *A General and Statistical Survey of the County of Cork* (1810), an encyclopaedic history of the county (available freely online), as interesting for his facts and figures as for his colourful opinions on the people of Cork. He thought, for example, that Cork women spent too much time lounging around and not getting enough exercise – ironic from a vicar who found time to write a 900-page book!

The picture-postcard view of Castletownsend is from the water, looking back on the Castle and the hill behind. Piercing the skyline are the Gothic pinnacles of St Barrahane's Church, built in the 1820s by the architect James Pain. Inside you will find artwork associated with the Somerville and Townsend families. St Barrahane's is perhaps best known for its three wonderful stained-glass windows by Harry Clarke (1889–1931). The nave window of saints Louis IX and Martin of Tours (dated 1921) is one of the finest examples of early twentieth-century Irish glass. In the porch, look out for an oar which washed ashore from RMS *Lusitania*, sunk by a German U-boat in 1915 with the loss of almost 1,200 lives. In the adjoining churchyard are the graves of Somerville and Martin.

Castletownsend is the perfect base for exploring the surrounding area by land and by water, including:

Sea kayaking, from Reen Pier on the far shore of Castlehaven. Paddle around the harbour in your own kayak, or contact Atlantic Sea Kayaking, who offer day and night tours of the beautiful coastline and beyond.

Whale watching, also from Reen Pier. Colin Barnes of Cork Whale Watch organises trips to spot whales off the coast. Book well in advance as spaces sell out quickly.

Rineen Forest Recreation Area (Rineen Woods), a 10-minute drive. There are shoreline trails here, lush woodland and ruined buildings. No charge for access and there's plenty of parking.

Union Hall and **Glandore**, a 15-minute drive. Union Hall is a quaint fishing village is known for its excellent smoked salmon, sold in supermarkets throughout the county and beyond. Nearby is the beautiful seaside village of Glandore, where the food at the Glandore Inn, looking out at the boats in the harbour, is highly recommended.

Drombeg Stone Circle, a 25-minute drive. Comprising seventeen standing stones and other ancient remains, this site is open to the public and has a commanding view of the sea.

Castle Freke, a 30-minute drive. Pronounced 'freak' by most locals, this is a popular spot for walks and cycles in old forestry. The fantasy Gothic castle, the home of many a Lord Carbery, is currently being restored.

IMAGES Below: St Barrahane's Church, Castletownsend. Opposite, top: The busy anchorage of Glandore. Opposite, bottom: Dark clouds gather over Drombeg Stone Circle.

CLONAKILTY

CLONAKILTY (*CLOICH NA COILLTE*). 'Clon' lies just beyond the radius of commuter towns for Cork city – and this is a blessing. It has a character independent of the city, an economy still defined by farming and tourism, and plenty of good old buildings that give it the feel of a prosperous market town. Richard Boyle (1566–1643), the 'great earl of Cork', founded Cloughnakilty (as it was then spelled) back in 1613 with a charter from King James I. The town's name derives from, in Irish, *Cloich na Coillte*, meaning approximately, 'stone castle of the woods'. On the eve of the Great Famine, almost 4,000 people lived here, but by 1960 this was down to just over 2,400; now it has risen again to around 4,700. Some remnants of the pre-Famine prosperity can be found in the grand townhouses surrounding the tree-lined Emmet Square (a rarity in West Cork).

Despite the falling population, a railway to Cork opened in 1886, and a great Catholic church – almost cathedral-like in its scale and setting – was added by the architect George Ashlin in the 1870s. For many years, the growing of sugar beet was an important local enterprise, with the produce taken by rail to Mallow. Old-world charms survived around here for a long time, not least in the Shannonvale mill just outside the town (now abandoned), which was served by a short horse-drawn railway branch as late as 1961.

The growing of crops is still more important in Clonakilty than in most other West Cork towns, as you will surely notice when some enormous farm machinery adds to the traffic jams. Emmet Square is a great place to escape the congestion, and on Friday mornings it also hosts the local Farmers' Market. The town is known for its black pudding, made to a recipe that has been a carefully guarded secret for over a hundred years. Colette Twomey's company now makes a range of puddings, sausages, and rashers – including in recent years vegetarian and vegan options! The visitor centre explores the long history of farming in the area, as well as giving you a chance to sample Twomey's award-winning products.

Clonakilty's pubs are renowned for their traditional music and singing. The biggest music festivals are the Street Carnival (in June), the Waterfront Festival (in August) and the International Guitar Festival (in mid-September).

The town is closely associated with Michael Collins (1890–1922), the leading figure of the Irish War of Independence (1919–1921) who was assassinated during the subsequent Civil War (1922–1923). Collins was born near Sam's Cross around 5km west of the town and lived for a while in a house on Emmet Square, where a statue now commemorates his life. Shortly before he was killed at Béal na mBláth, he made a visit back to Clonakilty and to his old home-place – the full details of which are explained at the highly recommended Michael Collins Centre.

Beyond the town, the many sights to see include:

West Cork Model Railway Village, at the eastern edge of the town. This favourite for children has been welcoming visitors for more than twenty years.

Inchydoney beach, a 10-minute drive. The great sandy beach at Inchydoney almost cuts off Clonakilty from the sea. It is often very busy in the summer.

IMAGES Below: A bronze statue of Michael Collins stands in Clonakilty's Emmet Square.
Opposite, top: Rock, sea and sand at Inchydoney beach.
Opposite, bottom: The West Cork Model Railway Village, an essential visit for any train enthusiast.

Ford Model T, Ballinascarty, a 10-minute drive. Here you can see a stainless-steel replica of the famous 'Model T' car, erected to commemorate the Ford family who came from the area.

Michael Collins birthplace, Woodfield (Sam's Cross), a 10-minute drive. There are old stone cottages here, which were burnt by British forces in 1921 and later rebuilt. The cottages are open to the public.

Michael Collins Centre, Castleview, a 10-minute drive. This award-winning museum is run by descendants of Collins. Their tours are highly recommended and include all the key sites including *Béal na mBláth*.

Galley Head and **Dundeady Castle ruins**, a 20-minute drive. Spectacular views of much of the south coast along with a large lighthouse.

Kinneigh round tower, Sleenoge, a 30-minute drive. One of Cork's hidden gems, well off the beaten track. Kinneigh (built c. 1200, 21m high) is the only round tower in Ireland to be partly hexagonal in plan. Surrounded by a lovely old churchyard.

COURTMACSHERRY

COURTMACSHERRY (*CÚIRT MHIC SEAFRAIDH*). Like many coastal towns in West Cork, Courtmacsherry is buzzing in the summer months and sleepy in the winter. The old landlord, the Earl of Shannon, improved the town to tempt visitors back in the 1830s, and he also built the present pier then. Courtmacsherry is best understood as just one part of the larger and exceptionally beautiful natural landscape of the Argideen estuary, stretching around 7km inland past the village of Timoleague to Inchy Bridge, an old stone bridge in dense woods. The river – the 'little silver stream' in Irish – is well known in fishing circles as one of the best sea trout rivers in the southwest. At low tide, almost the entire estuary is sand and mud, and a favourite spot for bird watching; at high tide, the reflections of Timoleague's medieval friary glisten in the water, and the fishing boats come and go. This sheltered inlet and its excellent agricultural hinterland have been attracting

IMAGES Opposite, left: The unusual medieval round tower at Kinneigh is partly hexagonal in plan.
Opposite, top right: Spectacular Galley Head and its lighthouse.
Opposite, middle right: A replica Ford 'Model T' at Ballinascarty.
Above: Timoleague's medieval friary. Taken on a sunny November day in 1960 by British tourist John Langford, the scene is unchanged today, more than 60 years later.
Below, left: Pretty road signage recalling the old railway system welcomes visitors to Courtmacsherry.
Below, right: Courtmacsherry's pier was built in the 1830s by the then Earl of Shannon.

humans to settle for a very long time. Timoleague stretches back to perhaps the seventh century, as its name suggests – Tigh Molaga, the house of St Molaga. You will notice in the area a large number of old buildings from times past, including ruined monasteries and castles (Monteen, for example, near Ballinascarty), as well as woodland (Ummera and many others) and dozens of elegant Georgian farmhouses.

Courtmacsherry is a one-street town, with colourful houses to one side and moored boats in the sea to the other. It is home to around 600 people, though this varies hugely by the season. You will find marked walks east of the town out to Wood Point. Look out along the way for the Fuchsia Walk, a serene one-hour marked loop trail. If you are looking for something a bit livelier after several days' fishing and walking, visit in August for the Harbour Festival and especially Regatta day. Nearby Timoleague also has a Harvest Festival around the same time. The local pubs are the perfect spots to learn more about the area's history and especially its maritime traditions; no doubt you will hear that there has been an RNLI lifeboat in Courtmacsherry for almost two centuries (one of the oldest in Ireland). Back in 1915, local men helped rescue survivors from the RMS *Lusitania* as it sank following a U-boat attack. One of the volunteers was Tim Keohane, whose son Patsy (1879–1950) made his name exploring the Antarctic on Scott's ill-fated *Terra Nova* expedition of 1910–1913.

A walk commemorating the former railway line now extends by the shore from Courtmacsherry to Timoleague. Here roadside steam locomotives ran from 1891 to 1961. The old railway ran within a couple of feet of the evocative ruins of Timoleague's friary, built around 1300. The ruins are open to the public, and inside you will see the former church itself, along with a dormitory, library, infirmary and an elaborate cloister. The bell-tower was added around 1500 during the time of Edmund de Courcy, Bishop of Ross; today its sea-dampened stones are covered with green moss and lichen, and it is home to the wildlife of the estuary. Sadly, the friary was burned, 'with all the towne' as the old records add, by English forces during the Confederate Wars in 1642. Of more recent religious history, the Church of Ireland church has a mesmerising interior of mosaic and marble in a Mughal/Indian style, partly funded by the Maharaja of Gwalior in the mid-1920s in memory of a medical doctor from the area.

From Courtmacsherry and Timoleague, there are many exciting things to see and do:

Atlantic Whale and Wildlife Tours, departing from Courtmacsherry. The south coast is teeming with wildlife, including minke and humpback whales, dolphins, and many others.

Gecko Adventures, also based in Courtmacsherry. Once you have walked the walks, take to the sea for windsurfing classes, kayaking and paddle-boarding.

Courtmacsherry Sea Angling Centre, departing from the pier. The waters off Seven Heads and the Old Head of Kinsale are known internationally for their excellent sea angling.

Sandy beaches, many to choose from within a 15-minute drive of Courtmacsherry. Dunworly is highly recommended and has rock pools and caves. Broadstrand is known as a safe beach for swimming.

IMAGES Top: The Argideen estuary with Timoleague's friary in the distance.
Bottom: A peaceful evening in Courtmacsherry.

KINSALE

KINSALE (*CION tSÁILE*). The first image that comes to mind when I think of Kinsale is of its rows of brightly coloured buildings set into the hills like the tiers of a wedding cake. Tying them together are a maze of steep, mostly one-way streets, the exact arrangement of which is still a mystery to me even after so many visits. Invariably they lead you to an unexpected historic building or vista – and this element of surprise is one of the joys of Kinsale. After all, this is a town with both a 'Higher O'Connell Street' and a 'Lower O'Connell Street'.

The best way to approach Kinsale is not on either of the main roads from the airport but along the small coastal routes that wind their way from Courtmacsherry. The landscape reveals itself with unusual, almost arcadian grandeur, and introduces Kinsale for what it really is: *Cionn tSáile*, 'the head of the briny water', the end-point of the River Bandon, one of the great rivers of Cork.

By West Cork standards, Kinsale is a big town, with a population of around 5,500 people. It is firmly within the commuter belt for Cork city. The busy marina and art galleries tell you of its recent economic success, and the *Shell Guide*'s description back in 1967 of a 'charming, decayed, old seaport' is hardly recognisable now. A sweeping bend in the river protects the town from the bad weather, and this natural advantage has long drawn settlers and shipping. There were monks here in the seventh century, Vikings in the ninth and Normans in the twelfth, when the port was known as Endilworth or Endelford.

The town turns up in every Irish history book for the Battle of Kinsale (1601–1602), when the Spanish briefly held power until disaster struck and the English forces blockaded the town and eventually drove them out. The siege led to the demise of the old Gaelic order. Almost a century later, James II landed here to try and retake the country from William of Orange, but after failure at the Battle of the Boyne, came back to Kinsale and departed Ireland, never to return.

In between all this drama of kings and battles, Kinsale served as one of Ireland's most important ports. Wine arrived from the south of France, and convoys of ships stopped off to prepare for transatlantic journeys (taking with them beef and butter). Only much later, and especially following the relocation of the British navy to Cork harbour, did the town go into a gradual decline until tourism developed in the nineteenth century.

In among Kinsale's narrow streets are many old buildings that recall this rich history. The Church of Ireland church of St Multose dates in part back to the thirteenth century, and Desmond Castle, towards the northern edge of the old town, was built in the sixteenth century. Nearby is the wonderful Market House from 1707, in an Anglo-Dutch style of architecture that speaks to the lucrative shipping links with the continent during that era.

Kinsale's countless small shops, cafés and restaurants are busy in the summer months, and there are endless events to choose from. Towards the end of October, there is a major jazz festival. If the crowds are too much, there is much to see beyond:

Summer Cove, less than 5 minutes' drive. A popular bathing spot in the summer, with a pub right by the water.

IMAGES Below: Kinsale's Market House dates from 1707.
Opposite, top: A colourful scene in Kinsale.
Opposite, bottom: Early morning on a winter's day in Kinsale.

Café
Milk Market Café
Stone Mad
Mother Hubbard's

Charles Fort, at Summer Cove, and James Fort, accessible via Kinsale bridge. James Fort was built first (c. 1603), with Charles Fort added in 1677. A must-see for any visitor. Charles Fort, in particular, is an exceptional example of military architecture. When the British left in 1922, the local IRA set fire to the fort.

Ballinspittal grotto, a 15-minute drive. In 1985, there were reports that the statue of Mary had come to life. Thousands descended on the grotto to see the miracle for themselves but most – it would seem – were left disappointed. You never know, you might be lucky.

Garretstown Strand, a 20-minute drive. On the western side of the Old Head, this is a favourite beach, with cliffs and big waves.

IMAGES Top: The ruins of Charles Fort, near Kinsale. Bottom: Big swells at Garretstown beach.

First published 2022 by The O'Brien Press Ltd,
12 Terenure Road East, Rathgar, Dublin 6, D06 HD27, Ireland.
Tel: +353 1 4923333; Fax: +353 1 4922777
E-mail: books@obrien.ie
Website: obrien.ie
The O'Brien Press is a member of Publishing Ireland.

ISBN: 978-1-78849-226-3

Cover and interior design by Tanya Ross

7 6 5 4 3 2 1
26 25 24 23 22

Printed by EDELVIVES, Spain.
The paper in this book is produced using pulp from managed forests.

Published in DUBLIN UNESCO City of Literature

Enjoying life with O'BRIEN obrien.ie

Picture credits:
Shutterstock: pages 3, 5, 7, 8, 9, 10, 13, 15 (bottom), 16 (bottom), 17, 18 (top and bottom right), 21 (top, bottom left and right), 22 (top right and bottom left), 25, 27, 28 (middle), 29 (top and bottom), 30 (top), 31, 32 (top and bottom), 35 (top and bottom), 37 (middle right), 38 (bottom), 39, 41 (top left), 43 (bottom right), 45 (top left and middle left), 46 (top), 49, 53 (top left, top right, bottom left and bottom right), 55 (top right), 57 (top, middle left, bottom left and bottom right) 59 (top left, top right, middle right and bottom), 61 (bottom), 63, 64 (top right and bottom), 67 (top, middle left, bottom left and bottom right), 69 (top right, middle left and bottom), 71 (bottom), 72 (middle and bottom), 73 (top), 74 (top), 75, 76, 87 (middle left), 89, 93 (bottom right), 94 (top and middle left), 96 (bottom), 99 (top, bottom left and bottom right), 101 (top and bottom), 102, 103 (top and bottom), 104 (top right), 107 (top and bottom), 109 (top and bottom), 111 (top and bottom).
Richard Butler: pages 6, 15 (top, middle left and middle right), 16 (top), 18 (bottom left), 21 (middle left), 22 (middle left and middle right), 26 (top and bottom), 28 (top), 30 (bottom), 33, 34, 37 (top, middle left and bottom right), 38 (top), 41 (top right, middle left, middle right and bottom), 43 (top, bottom left), 45 (top right and bottom), 46 (bottom), 51 (top, bottom left and bottom right), 55 (top left and bottom), 60, 61 (top), 64 (top left), 69 (middle right), 71 (top left, middle left, lower middle left, top right), 73 (bottom), 74 (bottom), 77 (top left, top right, middle, bottom), 78, 79 (top, bottom left, middle right, bottom right), 80 (top, bottom left, bottom right), 81, 82, 83 (top and bottom), 84, 85, 87 (top, bottom left and bottom right), 90 (top, middle and bottom), 91, 92, 93 (top, middle and bottom left), 94 (middle right), 96 (top), 97 (top left and top right), 99 (middle), 100, 104 (top left and middle right), 105 (bottom left and bottom right), 108.
John Langford: pages 22 (top left), 105 (top).